GUIDE TO NO GRANDCHILDREN

How to cope when our kids don't have kids –
Dealing with feelings and moving on with our lives

Emily Wells

Guide to No Grandchildren

Copyright © 2023 Emily Wells

Independently published 2023

CONTENTS

INTRODUCTION

"Do you have grandchildren?"

That innocent question is so easy to answer for most people over 50. "Yes!" they reply enthusiastically. And out come the photos and the anecdotes. The only tricky part for the person asking, is getting a word in edgeways – grandparents just *love* to talk about their grandchildren.

Since you are reading this book, though, your response may not come so readily. In fact, you might have come to dread being asked that question.

Because the answer for us is; no. We do not have grandchildren. We have an adult child, or more than one of them, but they either can't reproduce or they don't want to. And when we say as much, we've come to expect the awkward pause, the look of pity and the questioner's instant loss of interest in us.

We are not part of their club. We are the grandchildless. And there are more and more of us each year, as birth rates fall and young people increasingly see having a family as an option, not a given.

We long for grandchildren, but our kids are not parents and it doesn't look as if that's going to change. Maybe we took it for granted that one day there would be grandbabies. We may have planned for it, saved for it and, well, simply expected it.

Now we know differently, and the adjustment to our new reality can be a slow, painful and lonely one. What we pretty soon find out is that society in general, and people we know in particular, are not always sympathetic to our situation. In fact they can be careless of our feelings, dismissive of our concerns, and at times downright cruel.

And that's just trying to deal with some of the external problems. Inside, we may also be experiencing intense feelings, the like of which we may never have known before and might not have expected.

Sadness is often the principal emotion, a deep and persistent ache that we try in vain to banish. We grieve for the life we won't have and the grandchildren that will never exist. We might also feel anger, fear, shame and alienation. The catalogue of potential negative emotions is long, and a major focus of this book will be on identifying, coping with and working through those feelings.

Our relationships, especially with our children but also with family, friends and colleagues, may become a source of friction and difficulty. We wonder what to do with the heirlooms, the toys we saved, our family history. We might even wonder what the point of it all is, if our family line ends and our genes are no longer passed on.

So with that as the background, how can this book help? How do we navigate this experience; one that we didn't expect and passionately don't want? How do we survive the pain, the sadness, the sense of isolation? How do we keep ourselves mentally and physically well, and create a new identity for ourselves – one that offers meaning, purpose and comfort?

Answering those questions is the aim of this book. I've lived this experience for many years. I've done my time, and in order to write this book I've also done my research.

I'm retired now, but my background as a counsellor helps me understand the psychological pressures that come with having no grandchildren. And my experience as a writer means, I hope, that I can communicate effectively with you as we navigate this part of our lives.

Part One looks in detail at the experience of not having our own biological grandchildren. We'll consider the emotional impact, the social implications, the effects on our relationships and the toll it can take on us.

Part Two examines how we can heal ourselves and learn to live happy, purposeful lives despite this setback. I'll talk about mental health and emotional self care, including when and how to get professional help if you need it. About maintaining strong relationships, especially with our children. About ways to fill the gap in our lives, about what to do with the "stuff", and finally about our own legacy.

There will be **"Action Points"** throughout Part Two. You can use this book however you like, of course. Everyone is different. Some of you will want to devour the book at one sitting while others will dip into it, or read the bits that seem most important first.

But if you want a more structured approach, the Action Points are designed to help you work through your experiences, gently but effectively. There will be more about this in Part Two.

Hopefully you will not only reach a deeper understanding of yourself and what's happened to you, but also develop new techniques and ways of coping that will lead you towards a happier and more fulfilling life. It can be done!

In writing this book I've created a resource that I wish I'd been able to access when I started on this journey. It's time to end the stigma around the lack of grandchildren. We are here, we're important and we deserve to be heard.

MY STORY (BRIEFLY)

I'm a 65-year-old woman with adult children. Life's been pretty good to me, though there have been ups and downs, just as there have for most of us.

But I have a lot to be thankful for. I live comfortably in a safe, stable country. I have loving relationships. My health isn't bad, all things considered. I'm retired, and I have hobbies and activities that keep me busy.

And yet there's a gaping hole in my life, one that can't be filled by any of the above. A massive gap where one vitally important thing should be ....

My grandchildren.

I have no grandchildren. Some young people can't have babies and others don't want to, and my adult children represent both groups.

It's not going to change. The long years of hope have gradually faded away and now I'm left staring at the stark reality.

No one is ever going to call me Grandma. I will never experience the joy of holding a newborn grandchild. I am not a member of that massive, but exclusive, worldwide club of grandparents. That club whose membership is demonstrated every time a proud grandparent whips out the pics of the darling grandkids, or shares a story about something cute they said or did, or parades them in public, or breaks a date with us because they "have" to look after them all weekend.

My relatives have grandchildren, and my friends have them too. More and more over the years, I have felt like I'm on the outside looking in, my face pressed to the glass as I watch other people doting on little ones, sharing in their lives as they grow and celebrating all the usual childhood milestones.

How did this happen? Did I do something terribly wrong when I was raising my family? Have I somehow instilled a dislike of babies and children in my own kids?

I don't think so – but perhaps I'm deluding myself. I wanted to be a mother so much, and I was so thrilled to find myself expecting for the first time in my mid twenties. There had been a few indications that I might have trouble conceiving, so I felt especially lucky when it turned out not to be much of a problem to fall pregnant.

My children were very much wanted and cherished, and I believe on the whole they had happy childhoods. They tell me so, anyway.

It's been fifteen years now since the first of my friends excitedly told me "I'm going to be a grandmother!" That was the day I first realised how much I wanted that for myself.

And during the last decade and a half, the hope has gradually dwindled to nothing. I know now that it isn't going to happen. Meanwhile, pretty much all the women I know, family, friends and acquaintances, have become Grandmas.

Is your experience similar to mine? Did you carry a flame of hope that burned a little lower with each passing year, and eventually died? Or did you find out suddenly and dramatically?

However we came to this position, we're here now and goodness knows, we have suffered. We want help and support. A sympathetic ear, someone to show the way and convince us that life is still worth living and we can be happy and fulfilled, even without grandchildren.

We might look to the media for some support with our grandchildlessness, but we're not going to find it. Magazine articles with titles like "No Grandchildren? No Problem!" just trivialise the pain of our situation. A search of YouTube for the phrase "no grandchildren" brings up nothing that is relevant to us. Same result with an internet search.

As far as I can tell, my book is the first of its kind. There are vast numbers of self-help books and memoirs out there, covering pretty much all of human experience, except for this one. Extraordinary, isn't it?

I started writing this just for myself. We each have our own way of expressing ourselves, and writing's the one for me. I poured out my feelings, and thought about how I'd coped with them. Then I started to research what was happening in society, and how I had found myself in this position.

After a while, it occurred to me that other people might find some of this useful. I knew there were more and more of us who weren't going to be grandparents. And I also believed there was nothing like this book out there, because I'd already searched for it and drawn a great big blank.

And so a book was born. It's intended to be an honest examination of our situation, together with ideas for how we can take care of ourselves and heal from our experience.

There *is* life after no grandchildren. We *can* find joy and fulfilment. And hopefully this book will help to show the way.

I hope you find solace, support and practical help in the following pages, and I wish you peace and happiness in your life without grandchildren.

MEET DIANE, JEFF, TRIXIE AND VANESSA

Over the course of writing this book, I was privileged to talk to a number of people who share our experience of no grandchildren and who wanted to be part of the project. I asked them a lot of questions, some of them rather personal, and they were generous with their answers and their time. I'm grateful to all of them.

The four people whose stories you will meet in the book – Diane, Jeff, Trixie and Vanessa – have led very different lives from each other, and they have differing reasons for being without grandchildren. Between them they cover a lot of ground.

Their experiences will be found throughout the book, wherever they are relevant and can illustrate a particular issue.

My hope is that you'll find some similarities between your own situation and that of at least one of them. But even if you don't, I think they'll provide an enhanced sense of how widespread this problem is. So many people, from all walks of life, are struggling with not having their own grandchildren. We are not alone.

I have changed the names to protect their privacy.

So, without more ado, meet our grandchildless friends.

DIANE, 58.

Diane is single and works part-time in a florist's shop. She has one daughter, Saffron, who's 40 and also single.

"I only have the one child, a daughter. I called her Saffron because it's a beautiful shade of sunshine yellow, and also a delicious spice. Guess I was something of a hippy back in the day.

I had her very young, I was just eighteen. Her Dad and I didn't stay together for long after she arrived. I've often wondered if that's

---

why she despises the idea of having kids so much – she saw me struggling at times and doesn't want the same for herself. But even if we were poor, she was always safe and loved. I can't seem to get her to see that, though.

She played with dolls when she was small, just like any other little girl. It didn't occur to me till she was in her thirties that she might not have children. Looking back, all the signs were there. I just didn't see them.

Saffron's a free spirit, and I guess I was too, when I was younger. She loves to travel. Her relationships don't seem to last, and she's too busy saving the planet to think about having a child. We've talked about it, and she tells me the world is overpopulated – but I say, would one more baby really make that much difference to the future of mankind?"

JEFF, 67.

Jeff is a retired civil engineer. He's married, and his wife works as a book-keeper. They have two children, Marissa 38, and Joel 36.

Marissa recently told her parents that she is not interested in having a physical relationship with anyone. She has friends, but she's never dated. Joel is very absorbed in his career and though he has occasional girlfriends, he has no urge to settle down or start a family.

"I think this situation affects my wife more than me. I tend to get on with life and not dwell on anything. She sometimes tells me how sad and hopeless she feels, because our children aren't in relationships and she doesn't have a grandchild. I find it difficult to know how to respond. I struggle with seeing her crying, and while I want to support her, I don't want her to waste her life in regrets."

TRIXIE, 72.

Trixie is a widow, and a retired nurse. She keeps busy with hobbies and seeing friends, but she told me that she feels a great emptiness at the centre of her life.

She has three children. Paulette is 46 and married. She has struggled with infertility for fifteen years, undergoing several unsuccessful rounds of IVF treatment. She and her husband have considered adoption but feel they are too old now.

Suzanne is 43. She has a disability, and lives in sheltered housing. Trixie visits her frequently and offers as much support as she can.

Pete is 37. He lives with his long-term girlfriend but they've never mentioned having children. Trixie worries that his sisters' problems have put him off fatherhood.

"I would have loved a grandchild so much. It gets quite lonely now that I've lost my husband, and grandchildren would've been something to concentrate on, fill my time. There's always something going on with children, isn't there?

I fill in my time with hobbies, I knit for a charity and keep the garden looking nice. And I still help out with my disabled daughter, even though she has carers. My life is OK I suppose, I'm used to it. But it's not how I hoped it would be. Sometimes I wonder what it's all for."

VANESSA, 64.

Vanessa is married and works as a librarian. She has two children. Tom, 34, is gay and in a long-term relationship. Sophie (formerly Sam) is 31 and single.

"I don't know why both my children are LGBTQ. It was a shock to me and Kevin when we found out. They came out around the same time, when Tom was 18 and Sophie was 15. There's nobody else in the family who is gay or trans as far as I know. Of course, in the past people didn't talk about it so much."

I should mention here that the reasons for our lack of grandchildren are not always this obvious. Several of my other interviewees gave much vaguer explanations for their children not reproducing. So if you are thinking "Well at least they *know* why they don't have grandchildren," then rest assured that it's perfectly normal *not* to know, too.

I chose Diane, Jeff, Trixie and Vanessa in part because their situations are relatively straightforward – their children mostly have quite specific reasons for their childlessness. This may or may not be the case for you, and equally we may simply not know why ours don't or can't have children.

PART ONE

CHAPTER ONE

FOUR REASONS WHY OUR CHILDREN CAN'T HAVE CHILDREN

It's a source of immense sadness and pain to us if our children want to have babies, but can't. We need to deal with their sense of loss and grief as well as our own. This can be a tough road to travel and we need to do all we can to keep ourselves afloat, emotionally and mentally. At the same time we'll be doing our best to support them, too. It's a lot to deal with.

Before we get further into this subject, I want to say that the cause of not having children can't always be reduced to one specific thing. Often there are multiple factors at play. Some of them may be easy to identify, but there will frequently be subtle psychological pressures and tensions, as well as changing circumstances, that feed into what happens.

So it's helpful for us to be mindful of this as we consider our children's lack of babies. Also, there will probably be limits to how much they are willing to discuss with us, or they might try to fob us off. We'll look more at this in the later chapter on how to talk to our children and others.

Meanwhile, I've divided up this and the next chapter into common causes of lack of grandchildren. This is for convenience and ease of understanding, but bear in mind as you read that there may well be more than one issue and it's unlikely to be as straightforward as it seems here.

Let's start this chapter by looking at some of the reasons why your adult child may not be able to have a baby.

1. Infertility

This is a tragic and surprisingly common reason for no grandkids. According to the US Department of Health and Human Services, around 9% of men and 11% of women have experienced fertility problems. These figures are similar in other parts of the Western world.

So this means that one in every ten would-be grandparents is denied their heart's desire – a grandchild – through that offspring's infertility. That is a lot of people. Of course, if people have more than one child this may not be the end of the grandparent road for them. But still, imagine the amount of heartbreak for so many parents whose hearts bleed for their son or daughter.

The son may not be physically able to father a child. The daughter may not be capable of conceiving a baby, or perhaps she can't carry a pregnancy to term. Sometimes it's a combination of fertility problems involving both members of the couple.

Trixie's elder daughter has been through this -

> *"It's been so difficult for my daughter. She wanted a baby so much. She's given up trying now, and I don't blame her, but my hopes died when she told me. She has a little dog, and she dresses it up and makes a big fuss of it. That tugs on my heartstrings."*

And as time goes on without a baby appearing, we have to acknowledge that fertility declines naturally with age, especially for women. There is also an established trend towards having children later in life. Far more young women these days don't contemplate motherhood until they are in their thirties, which inevitably feeds into fertility issues for some. It can be a long-drawn-out process with hope gradually fading as the years go by.

There is also the situation where it's the partner of our son or daughter who has issues with their fertility. And this can bring its own share of difficult feelings for us. Resentment perhaps, anger, or an uncharitable wish for our child to "cut their losses" and try again with someone else.

If we ourselves have experienced any difficulty in having children, emotional wounds can be reopened for us. It can seem like a terrible pattern repeating itself across the generations.

In this situation, I believe having someone to talk to about our feelings is especially important. Counselling and therapy can most certainly have an important role, but so too can very good friends (especially if they have a similar experience) or a trusted, wise person in your community.

Don't struggle on for years without help, especially if you think your own mental health is having a negative effect on your relationship with your child, or with your own partner.

2. No partner

We may wonder why our adult child is not in a relationship. They're attractive, well-educated and have a good job, so why no partner? They may be "playing the field", but as they enter their late twenties we might feel that's gone on long enough.

Or, it may sadly be all too obvious why they are not paired up. Perhaps they are painfully shy, or have always had difficulty making friends. Perhaps they're suffering from anxiety or depression, and can't get out to meet people. Maybe they even suffer with an issue such as substance abuse.

Whatever the reason, our children are probably not going to be planning a pregnancy if they're not in a stable relationship. There are exceptions, of course. For example, some young women decide they'd rather take on the burdens of single parenthood than face a childless future. But generally, no partner = no babies.

This can be frustrating for us. We love our kids, so why doesn't someone else? On the other hand, this is perhaps a situation that offers more hope than many others. It's not unknown for people to get together in their late twenties, thirties or forties, even if they have missed out on the typical teenage and early twenties dating scene.

I think the key to negotiating this scenario is to keep out of it as much as possible. No nagging, no setting them up with the "suitable" offspring of our friends, and no trying to force them into social situations which may be uncomfortable or frightening for them.

Instead, we can be open to listening if they want to talk about it, as always. And we can support them as much as possible if there's a specific problem that's causing the lack of romantic engagement. Let's try to help with the root cause, such as depression; not the symptom, which is not wanting to date.

There is one more potential cause here that also crosses into the LGBTQ+ section of this chapter. Some people are asexual, or "ace". They just don't experience much, if anything, in the way of sexual attraction, and so their motivation to find a romantic partner is greatly diminished. They might be sociable and have plenty of platonic friends, but no actual partner.

If you wonder if this might be the case with your child, you may like to read the next section about LGBTQ+ people for further information and ideas.

3. LGBTQ+

You have probably seen this acronym, which stands for Lesbian, Gay, Bisexual, Trans, Queer (or Questioning), and the + is for everyone not included in the other groups, for example Asexual (see the section above). Essentially, everyone who is not heterosexual or "straight is included under the LGBTQ+ umbrella. There are other versions of these initials out there, so please forgive me if this is not the one you are most familiar with.

You may have known for some time, or at least considered the possibility, that your child was not straight. In this case, you've probably already considered the impact this may have on their decision or ability to have their own children.

Or it might be new to you – perhaps your child just recently came out. In which case your attention may be more focused on how to support your child, rather than on adapting to no grandchildren. There is a lot of useful information on the internet for parents of LGBTQ+ children. If you type "my son is ....." or "my daughter is ....." into a search engine, you will find websites that provide help and support. It's beyond the scope of this book to go further into the subject, but as always, if your mental health is being severely affected, do seek professional support from your doctor or a therapist.

This is Vanessa's experience -

"When Sophie started taking hormones it dawned on me that she was altering her fertility, maybe permanently. I don't know if it's reversible. In any case she seems happy being female. Children are not an option for her any more.

Tom has never expressed any interest in becoming a father. And to be honest, I'm not sure how I would feel about a child being brought up by two gay men. That probably sounds terrible, and I know you're not meant to say that kind of thing. It's not that I don't think they'd provide a safe and loving home, either. I don't know, it's all too complicated."

So, if you know your son is gay or your daughter is a lesbian, for example, what impact is this going to have on your hopes for grandchildren?

It depends on the particular situation. Trans people who take hormones may limit their fertility. Lesbian women always have the option of using a donor for pregnancy and can raise a child in a loving and stable relationship with another woman. Gay men can also provide such a loving and stable home, but actually having a child is much more difficult for them. A few gay couples do use a surrogate to have their own children, but it's a challenging and expensive path to take.

This situation is one that often provokes a response of "Why me?" or "Did I do something wrong?" in parents. If you have a strong faith and it is one that condemns homosexuality, that will be an additional factor for you to deal with. Or if you have particularly conservative values, or come from a family that holds such values, this again can cause major issues.

I won't go into these matters here – they are very much for the individual to decide. But I do want to make the point that, increasingly, science shows that sexual orientation is an innate part of who we are. It's not a lifestyle choice, or something that can be "cured". It is not caused by something that you did or did not do. It's part of your child, and hopefully you still love that child and want to support them.

4. Disability

Having a disabled child brings us all kinds of loss. Our child might never be able to live an independent life, and one result of this that we might have to face is that they will never have a child of their own.

If their disability has been apparent from birth or early childhood, we may have had plenty of time to adjust to the reality of their future. But if the disability is of recent date - for example a genetic condition that only reveals itself in the teens or twenties, or from an accident of some kind

– then we may now be acknowledging the lack of grandchildren for the first time, along with a whole host of other new limitations for our child.

Of course, not all conditions rule out having a baby. But some more profound levels of disability clearly do. It can be hard to accept this, sometimes – we may feel that with enough support our child could still become a father or mother.

In these situations, I think it's important to consider how realistic these dreams might be. In particular, look at it from the child's point of view. Every child deserves parents who are capable of looking after them properly. Perhaps your son or daughter could technically have a baby, but would this really be in the best interests of the child? Would you honestly want to take on effectively raising that child, on top of what might be considerable caring duties you already have?

There are no easy answers and each case is different. Allow yourself to grieve what might have been. Treasure your son or daughter as they are. Acceptance is hard, but it is the road to peace.

In the next chapter we'll look at situations where it's a matter of "won't" rather than "can't".

CHAPTER TWO

FOUR REASONS WHY OUR CHILDREN DON'T WANT CHILDREN

In the last chapter we considered four reasons why our kids might not be able to have babies of their own. This chapter is for when our children remain childless by choice.

Those who choose not to have children sometimes describe themselves as "childfree". There is currently something of a social movement encompassing childfree status, with websites, a Reddit community and so on.

Here, we'll look at some of the main reasons why they might want to remain childfree. As with the last chapter, this is a simplified overview, but hopefully it will provide some insight.

From our standpoint, these reasons can be hard for us to process. We probably get, and sympathise with, infertility or disability as a cause of no grandchildren, but *choosing* to be childless? Why would they decide to be childfree when they could perfectly well have a baby? What is *wrong* with them??

Our reactions are completely understandable, but they don't get us very far in communicating with our offspring or accepting their decisions. So, let's break it down and look at the various reasons why they might be making these choices.

1. World overpopulation and climate change

A recent article (July 2020) in The Guardian newspaper, entitled "Why a generation is choosing to be child free", encapsulates some of the arguments for not bringing children into the world. Talking about the extinction of species on our planet, and the dangers of carbon emissions, the writer concludes "we know that the biggest contribution any individual living in affluent nations can make is to not have children."

And many young people now feel this way. Activists like the climate campaigner Greta Thunberg have profoundly affected the way children, teenagers and those in their twenties think about the future of the planet, and their place in it. This undoubtedly feeds into increased awareness of the impact having a baby has on the environment, and it's led a good number of people to question their choices around their fertility.

This might be OK with us if they were just deciding to limit their families. "By all means, have only two children, or even just one," we want to say to them. But in many case it goes further and babies are off the agenda completely. Often this will not be the only factor behind our child's decision to be childless, but it can be a profound moral basis for the decision and one that's difficult to argue against.

Here's Diane's experience with her daughter Saffron -

"Saffron's life is all about saving the world. She recycles, she cooks from scratch and all her clothes come from second-hand sources. Pretty much every time we meet up, she tells me how overpopulation is destroying the planet, and how more people should avoid having children. I'm scared that she's had her tubes tied and doesn't want to tell me."

2. Career and travel

I've grouped these two together because, while they are not necessarily linked, they are clear and specific reasons for not wanting children. "I'm wedded to my career" or "I can't be tied down when I love to travel." Have you heard either of these?

The ability to travel may be tied up with the notion of freedom, and perhaps this is what our child is trying to express here. Being dedicated to a time-consuming career is also a kind of freedom – freedom from domestic distractions and responsibilities.

In a way, our child using one of these reasons for no babies can be a kind of backhanded reward for our achievement in raising them. We have independent, successful children. Which of us didn't aspire to our son or daughter having a fulfilling, absorbing career? And which of us would have objected to our teenagers wanting to "see the world?"

But we thought they would find a way to combine the career with parenthood; and we expected that the travel bug would wear itself out after a few years. Apparently, we were wrong.

And so we are victims of our own success and have to accept the unintended consequences of having bright, hard-working, ambitious children, who are citizens of the world. Isn't it ironic, as the song says?

3. Fear

This one is a catch-all category, covering all manner of reasons for not having babies. I'll take the issues one at a time.

Fear of pain, and of changes to the body

Our daughters may have a genuine fear of the birth process. Those of us in the developed world are lucky to live at a time when pain is a rare event for many children. They may never even have felt the dentist's drill, let alone experienced a bad accident, a serious illness, or any other pain-filled misfortune. And so even pregnancy, with its nausea, tiredness, aching legs and so on, may seem a scary prospect. Let alone actually expelling a small human being from your body.

And there is now so much pressure on young women to be physically gorgeous and desirable. Many "imperfections" can be fixed these days, if not by rigorous attention to diet and exercise then by surgery. Is your nose too big, are your boobs too small? No problem! The doctor will fix it for you.

So the idea of risking stretch marks and sagging breasts might be genuinely repulsive to some young people. They've put an awful lot of effort and sometimes money into looking perfect, after all. Why spoil all that?

Those of us who had our babies at a time when giving birth seemed more natural, and when the effects on our bodies were looked on as a small price to pay for bringing life into the world, might see these objections as trivial or as manifestations of vanity and self-obsession. But we were never exposed to the intense pressure from the media and social websites that our children experience daily. Our own physical imperfections were just something we lived with.

The gulf between the generations is especially wide here, it seems.

Fear of lack of money

Here is another big generational shift – expectations for the sort of lifestyle we take for granted.

We are shaped by our early experiences. If we grow up in a comfortable, relatively affluent home, then that lifestyle will seem "normal" to us for the rest of our lives. For many people, their standard of living has risen very noticeably over the last fifty years. As a result many of our children have been raised in luxury, by historical measures.

In contrast, some of us grew up in what would today be considered poverty, though at the time it was just normal life. My childhood home had no central heating or washing machine. Our furniture was generally second-hand, and much of my wardrobe was hand-me-downs. The family holiday was a week at the seaside in a boarding house. I can still remember when we first acquired a TV and a small, ten-year-old car.

Only my father had a paid occupation (my mother, of course, worked at least as hard as he did but her job inside the home didn't attract wages then any more than it does today). And all of this was commonplace for a middle-class British family at the time.

Compare this with the expectations of people currently in their twenties and thirties. Foreign holidays are the norm. Eating out or grabbing a coffee is not a treat but a weekly, if not daily, necessity. New clothes, new furniture, the latest phone - all expected. If you shop second-hand you're either an environmental extremist or a freak.

At the same time, some demands on resources undoubtedly do cost much more than they did years ago. Rents in cities, for example, are sky-high. Few people can afford to own and run a car in their twenties, which was commonplace for us. And wages have not always kept pace with prices. So a combination of big expectations in some areas, and a genuine reduction of spending power in others, certainly puts a strain on our children's bank balances.

Articles in the media emphasise the huge financial cost of raising a child from birth to eighteen. Young people absorb these messages, and since they are unwilling to live the way their parents and grandparents did, they are legitimately discouraged from having children by the expense. They assume both parents will need to work in order to afford their home and lifestyle, and they can foresee the strain that's going to put on them and their finances.

The older generation can offer to help with some expenses, if they are in the fortunate position to be able to afford that. But it can be hard to convince your child to have the baby first and figure out how to pay for it later.

Fear of damage to relationship

It's increasingly normal for couples to look to each other not only for a source of companionship, sex and financial security, but also as a best friend. The young couple may not live near family, and so the support that once came organically from being near parents and siblings is lost. Clearly defined roles ("she does the cooking, he does the DIY") are blurred – I'm not saying this is a bad thing, by the way! Media portrayals of perfect couples "in love forever" feed this narrative of finding "The One" who is your soulmate.

All this puts great pressure on the marriage or partnership. Anything that threatens this primary relationship can be perceived as dangerous.

And research has certainly shown that having a baby can put great strain on the parents. A 2019 study looked at 2,000 new parents during the first year of their baby's life. It showed that a third of them experienced relationship problems and a fifth actually split up. Common reasons for the separation included constant arguments, lack of intimacy, tiredness and poor communication.

So perhaps it's understandable when our children don't want to jeopardise their most important relationship. We can offer them as much support as possible, but still, many of them will be reluctant to accept emotional support from a generation whose experience seems so far removed from theirs.

And if they live on the other side of the country (or even the world) there will in any case be a limit to how much that support means to them in practical terms.

Fear of having a baby with a disability

Some of our children have grown up with a sibling, or other close family member, who is disabled. In many cases this has affected them deeply, despite our best efforts to give them a normal childhood. And one way this might show itself, is through worry that any child they have might also be disabled.

If there is a genetic history linked to a specific condition then genetic counselling is available. The prospective parents will be given a clear view of the risks and can go on to make an informed decision that seems right for them. That decision might be not to have children.

But sometimes there isn't a genetic risk and their disabled relative's condition was caused by something else. In this case, on the face of it our child should be no more concerned than anyone else about having a baby with health problems.

It doesn't always work that way, though. Many people go into pregnancy without giving much thought to the risks of not having a perfect baby. And for the vast majority this confidence is justified.

Someone who has grown up around disability may have a different perspective, though. They might know intellectually that they are extremely likely to have a normal, healthy child. But they still might be very scared of that tiny risk.

Trixie has experienced this with her son -

> "My son's scared of having children in case they have the same disability as his sister. We never really found out why she has this condition. It doesn't seem to be genetic but he won't take the chance."

This is a heartbreaking situation, where the misfortune of one generation causes ongoing problems in the next. Sometimes counselling may help, but that's a decision for our child to make. All we can really do is be there for them and support their choices, however hard it may be.

4. Just don't like kids

Many of us grew up expecting to have children as part of the natural order of things. And at some point, maybe in our late teens or early twenties, maybe later, we reached a point where we really *wanted* to have a baby. It wasn't always the perfect time, we weren't necessarily completely ready, but we just *knew*.

So it can come as quite a shock when we realise that our children don't feel that way at all. For them, having a child isn't an instinct or a biological necessity, but simply a lifestyle choice.

And, given all the other reasons for not having children that we've looked at above, they may be quite happy deciding against that particular lifestyle. They will tell us that they don't feel maternal or paternal and we can forget becoming grandparents, as far as they are concerned.

Or maybe their partner feels this way. Trixie says -

> *"My son's girlfriend doesn't want children. If I'm completely honest, I wish he'd break up with her and find another girl who does want to be a mother. I wouldn't be sad to see the back of her. There, I've said it. Aren't I a horrible person?"*

It's true that not everyone loves babies, or enjoys the company of small children. Some people have always decided against parenthood on these grounds. But now, it feels like an epidemic of anti-kid sentiment is sweeping over our young people. Where did this widespread dislike of children come from?

Perhaps it's that our offspring are hardly out of childhood themselves. Pretty much everyone in developed countries is in full-time education until they are 18, and a very high proportion go on to college or university, thereby prolonging their dependence on their parents until they reach at least 21.

And it's now common for young adults, especially young men, to live with their parents for much of their twenties and even beyond. Our generation was out of there and into our own place straight after college, and college itself was a stepping-stone to full independent adult life. Theirs seems happy to come back home and stay in the nest indefinitely. Not for nothing are they called the "boomerang generation".

Food, fashion, leisure activities – all these used to be clearly differentiated between adults and children. Now everyone wears much the same clothing if they're five, 15 or 25. People continue to go to burger bars and visit Disneyworld well into adulthood. Computer games, skateboarding, fizzy drinks – these are commonplace across the generations now.

And other markers of adulthood, like starting a long-term career with one company, buying a car or taking on a mortgage, are either postponed till the thirties or forties, or simply don't happen. Even marriage is not nearly as common as it used to be.

If our children don't feel grown-up, they are unlikely to consider themselves ready for parenthood. They may get there eventually, but it will be at the cost of their most fertile years. And even as we continue to hope, we know that our prime grandparenting time is slipping away. How much fun is it really going to be, if a grandchild comes along when we're 80?

Instead of having children, a lot of young people are taking on pets. Dogs seem especially popular, with particular breeds coming in and out of fashion. French bulldogs and pugs seem to be all the rage at the moment (and with their big eyes and squashy faces, they look remarkably like babies - at least, as much as a dog can!).

Vanessa is experiencing this -

"Tom isn't interested in children. He and his partner have recently got two chihuahuas. I suppose that's their family. I am not interested in being a dog's Grandma, though."

This trend may even lead to our kids, who probably know we want grandchildren even if we've never explicitly told them, introducing their animals to us as "grandpuppies" or "grandcats".

Some of us might find this endearing and decide that if that's the closest we're getting to a real grandbaby, we'll take it. On the other hand we might find it ridiculous or insulting. In that case, I suggest you don't put up with the "Grandma to a dog" narrative. Just tell them, politely but firmly, that you prefer them not to use that name in relation to their pets.

In the last chapter we looked at causes of our children not being able to have babies, and in this one we considered four broad strands of reasons why our children may choose not to become parents. There are others – I don't pretend that this is an exhaustive list. Perhaps your child has given you an explanation that hasn't been covered here.

Whatever the reason, the reality is the same. We don't have a grandchild. In the next chapter we'll look at the potential minefield involved in talking to our children about the situation.

References

Guardian newspaper, 25 July 2020, "Why a generation is choosing to be child-free", Sian Cain

Independent newspaper, July 22 2021, "Majority of new parents admit to being clueless"

CHAPTER THREE

FRIENDS, FAMILY, ALIENATION

Long, long ago, or so it seems now, each of us started our family. The pregnancy, the birth, the early years – it can seem like a dream these days, but it did happen. Some of us repeated this pattern, maybe more than once, and some stopped after the birth of our first child.

We were now parents. We met other new parents, and renewed friendships with old pals who were also "expecting". We felt a special bond with sisters and cousins who were at the same stage of life. They all understood how we felt and knew the rhythms of our daily existence – the ups and down, the joys and the difficulties.

These were comfortable and mutually supportive relationships, and often we felt they would last us a lifetime. They saw us through the tumultuous teenage years, and we all waved our kids off to college, or to the world of work, with the same mixed feelings of wistfulness and relief. Happy to know we'd done a good (or good enough, at least) job of parenting, and sad to realise those days were over.

Then maybe there were some child-free years. We might still be working outside the home, and ageing parents may have begun to pose problems for us, but still – we were in our middle-aged prime and life was fine.

And then one day, we received an excited phone call from one of these women we'd been so close to. Or perhaps she made an announcement at a family gathering.

"I'm going to be a grandmother! Jane/John is expecting! We're thrilled!!!" Or some other version of these words. We've gone on to hear them so many times since, they've kind of blurred into one generic announcement.

And we were thrilled too, on their behalf. For perhaps the first time, we started to consider what it would be like to say these things ourselves. We wondered if our own child might be considering pregnancy. Our kids being in serious relationships began to take on a new significance.

We discover that the Grandma-to be is perhaps rather bound up in this new stage of her life, and maybe she's not quite as available as she once was for phone calls or lunch dates. And once her grandbaby arrives, she is *really* busy. We realise that we haven't actually seen her or heard from her in weeks. And then, months.

This has been Diane's experience -

"My sisters have grandchildren. They are both younger than me, too. I'm happy for them, but it cuts like a knife sometimes, seeing them surrounded by little ones. They used to tell me all the time that Saffron would change her mind and have a baby, she just needed to meet the right man ... but I notice those comments have dried up the last few years."

More grandchildren start arriving in our social circle. The new grandmothers are understandably besotted, and we get to see more and more photos of new babies and later, toddlers and pre-schoolers. They talk a lot about them, and don't seem as interested as they once were in our own news.

At parties and family get-togethers, the grandparents start to congregate and swap stories of their new lives. We might listen politely, but we have nothing to contribute. That dull cousin we always used to avoid starts looking like our main option for someone to talk to.

We've been excluded. *They* are now members of a new club, and we are not invited. However much we still care, whatever we say to show nothing's changed, they know different. And deep in our hearts, we know, too.

Diane again -

"Of course, my sisters' grandchildren have brought them closer together. I used to be big sis, the one they'd come to with problems. But nowadays I seem to have nothing much to offer, and they turn to each other instead of to me."

If we have a particular reason for our grandchildlessness, and it's one our social circle can't understand or doesn't approve of, this can make life even more fraught. Vanessa tells us -

"It's been very difficult for me with family. Some of my relatives are devout Christians and they don't believe homosexuality exists, let alone being trans. They say it's a lifestyle choice. I can't face arguing with them about it, and they are not tolerant of people like Sophie and Tom, so I find it easiest to avoid them. It's made my social life very hard, though. I no longer go to all kinds of family events that I used to enjoy."

The years pass and the gulf widens. We might lose touch with a friend we thought would be there for ever. We might start to avoid the most challenging of the family parties – the baby showers, the christenings, the first birthday parties. Christmas cards, with their family photos and

Round Robins, become a source of anguish instead of festive joy, and we dread their arrival.

The men in our lives can be all too aware of the change. This is Jeff's perspective -

"My wife used to be very social. She'd set up all kinds of dinner parties and get-togethers, sometimes to the extent that I wished she'd dial it back a bit. That's all changed now though. We lead very quiet lives these days."

Wow. This is grim. How on earth did we get here?

Is this your experience? Have some of these things happened to you, or are they beginning to happen?

Maybe it's not this bad for you. Yes, some of your relatives and friends are grandparents, but plenty aren't. Or if they are, they don't obsess over their grandkids to this extent. You still have adequate social contact that doesn't revolve around grandchildren.

If so, you are fortunate. You can probably keep things in perspective, and you still have a social life and maybe a support system that you can enjoy and rely on.

But others are not so lucky. It's not that unusual for literally *everyone* in our social group to be a grandparent except for us. It's not that rare to be the only one among siblings who has no grandchildren. And this can be very, very difficult to deal with.

Some of us cope by withdrawing from society. This is healthy enough in the short term, probably – the idea of "going on retreat" has a long and noble history. But when it becomes normal for us then problems can follow.

We are designed to be social creatures and live in groups. We need friends and peers to function at our best. Isolation can lead us into a low mental state including depression, and that is not good for us.

If you're suffering like this, please know that you are not alone. Others are in the same situation. That can be hard to believe, since our everyday experience tells us we're the only ones in the world who are in this position. But that is simply not true.

In the second half of the book we'll look in detail at ways to cope with isolation and alienation of all types, including the kind brought on be being the only person in your social circle without grandchildren.

But meanwhile, know that others are in the same boat as you. You are not alone, and there are ways forward. Hang in there.

HOW OTHER PEOPLE SEE US

Do you ever wonder what your friends and family think of you these days? How about colleagues, your hairdresser, even random strangers that you interact with only once?

Maybe they see you differently, as a result of you not having grandchildren.

And, short of asking them and getting a straight answer (an unlikely scenario most of the time, I think you'll agree) you'll never find out for sure.

Of course, we can't truly know what's going on inside someone else's head. We can only infer and deduce – from what they say, from what they don't say, from their body language, from the tone of their voice.

And often, we get it wrong. Often, what we perceive as a slight or a rejection, as pity or contempt, has little or nothing to do with us. They are having a bad day, they're in pain or discomfort, they just had a row with someone or they are preoccupied and not thinking about us at all.

So, please bear all that in mind as you read through this chapter. We need to do our best not to take things personally. We'll be happier for it, and there may be fewer misunderstandings with people we care about.

Having said all that, it's true that status, pecking orders and power structures exist within social interactions. And we might be feeling pretty sure that our position in a hierarchy has changed.

Maybe you sense your relatives once saw you as a strong competent woman and mother, central to the extended family group; and now you've been relegated to the sidelines, along with the maiden aunt and the never-married cousin.

Perhaps you fear you're being left out of things – no longer invited to get-togethers, missing out on phone calls from friends, not kept up-to-date with the family news?

Well, possibly so. And then again, perhaps not. Relationships change, and regardless of our status regarding grandchildren, some friendships fade over time and some family connections can weaken as the years pass.

On the other hand, when our close friends or relatives have grandchildren and we don't, there's no doubt this alters the dynamic between us. When our sister announces that her umpteenth grandchild is on the way, and we're still longing for our first one, it's hard to avoid feelings of envy or resentment. And negative feelings can sully the best relationships.

A friendship may end, or your bond with a sibling may weaken more than you expect. This can be incredibly painful. In Part 2 we'll look at what you can do, and how to cope, when this happens. But first, we will look at the signs and try to work out what's going on.

So, how do we tell if it's our imagination, or we really are drifting apart? Let's break it down.

It's not us, it's them

Some people do change quite radically when they become grandparents, especially if they have been very wrapped up in their children previously and haven't worked outside the home, or if they have few interests and hobbies.

Some women, in particular, throw themselves into the role of grandmother to the exclusion of pretty much everything else. They revel in their new status, spend as much time as possible with their grandkids, and generally become "Grandma" to the nth degree.

There's nothing objectively wrong with this. People are entitled to live their lives the way they choose, after all. But from our point of view, this all-encompassing adoption of the grandparent role makes it difficult for us to sustain a friendship. It's just too much for us to bear.

If you have do a relationship with this kind of person, it may well have been based on both of you having similar-aged children. Perhaps you were at maternity classes together, or your children became friends in kindergarten. It may feel like a very close relationship, but ask yourself this – to what extent is this friendship about a coincidence of circumstances, rather than actual liking?

Sadly, friendships like this may not survive the arrival of your friend's grandchildren. Here are some signs it's not going well -

- You make all the effort to stay in touch. She seldom or never phones or messages you.
- You make plans to meet, and she breaks them, often at the last minute. Or even worse, she "forgets" to turn up.
- She doesn't remember your birthday, though she always used to.
- When you are together she shows little or no interest in you or your life.
- You're not well, and she doesn't follow up to see if you've recovered.
- She's insensitive about your lack of grandchildren. She might even use it as an opportunity to dominate the conversation as she talks about her own. Often this can be the last straw for us.

Even in cases where you have outside interests in common - perhaps you met at a pottery class, or through work – this may not be enough to carry the friendship on. In general though, in this case there may be more hope for salvaging the situation. You can always put the friendship "on hold" for a while, and see if her infatuation with grandparenthood wears off a bit in the face of the reality. Babies and small children are hard work, after all, however delightful they may be.

Is this easier for men? Maybe so, in general. Jeff seems to cope pretty well, though there's a hint that he might be holding back his deeper feelings -

> "The men I play golf with occasionally produce photos of their grandchildren, or mention an event involving them. I think that sort of thing is worse for my wife – her friends all seem to be doting grandmothers who talk about their grandchildren all the time. I find such conversation boring, for the most part. But sometimes I suppose I do feel a twinge of envy. Best not to dwell on it, though."

Work

Relationships with colleagues are usually different from the ones described above, and with regard to your status at work there might even be some upside to your lack of grandchildren. Within many workplaces, grandparenthood is a sign of being over the hill. You can avoid being pigeon-holed as "a Grandma, and therefore past it".

Naturally, your actual line of work will be a major factor here. If you're an engineer you may run less risk of exposure to grandchild conversation than if you work in a nursery school.

If you are unfortunate enough to be employed alongside lots of grandparents, it may be difficult to get away from endless grandchild-based chatter.

Vanessa says -

> "At work people pass round photos of their grandchildren, and talk about them endlessly. It's so boring, and sometimes it's hurtful too. I keep my head down and try to avoid getting involved. I think I've developed a reputation as stand-offish and remote, but it's easier than having to be involved in their conversations."

This can be especially challenging to deal with – you can't usually avoid people in a work setting. Nor can you reasonably complain to management about their conversation! Sometimes people find the grandparent chat so difficult, they look for a new job. You could bear that in mind as an option if you dread going in to work every day.

Strangers

Even complete strangers can take the wind out of our sails with random comments and questions that presuppose we have grandchildren.

"Are you visiting your grandchildren?" enquires the girl on the desk as we check into a hotel room.

"Spending the holidays with your grandkids?" asks the woman doing our nails.

"I've got six grandchildren now! How about you?" says the complete stranger standing next to us as we wait for a train.

The problem with these unprovoked attacks is that *we're* not prepared for the question, and *they're* making a very big assumption. They expect us to respond to these overtures with enthusiasm, so when we stutter, turn red or avert our eyes, they're shocked. The whole situation becomes thoroughly uncomfortable for all concerned.

This is the easiest situation to manage, though. You just need a couple of phrases that you can use, confidently, whenever you find yourself cornered. We'll try some ideas out in part 2.

CHAPTER FIVE

HOW THE MEDIA SEE US

"No Grandkids? No Problem!" proclaims the title of a recent magazine article. (By the way, this article was written by a woman who is herself a grandmother. Of course.)

That is so wrong. It *is* a problem. *We* have that problem. How dare they treat us like this?

But that headline is symptomatic of the way we are portrayed in the media on a regular basis. We are not entitled to grandchildren, they tell us (so far, I agree). Therefore, we are also not entitled to feel sad, or angry, or in fact, anything at all, if we don't have them. We should buck up and stop whining.

I strongly disagree. Goodness, this kind of thing makes me so angry!

On the other hand, articles like this one, annoying though they may be, are a rarity. That's because we're largely invisible. *Being* a grandparent is what it's all about.

In the same way that motherhood has never been so prized as it seems to be right now, so grandparenthood is also seen as a superior state of being. It's something to boast about and feel proud of, rather than just the normal consequence of having children that it's been for most of human history.

As we've seen, the media - by which I mean TV, films, radio, newspapers and magazines, and the internet - is generally not very interested in us as non-grandparents. For a start, they can't sell us anything. Grandparents will buy all sorts of items for their grandchildren. Adverts for toys, games, clothes, books and treats can legitimately be targeted at older people who have disposable income and want to spoil the grandchildren in their lives.

But us? Well, as a result of no grandchildren we might spend a bit more on some things, for example on our hobbies or pets. Perhaps some of us travel more. But that's all rather vague and provides nothing the advertisers can get their teeth into.

While the media is broadly sympathetic to people who can't have children, reflecting society's view, in general they are not at all sympathetic towards us. Hence the magazine pieces with bracing, no-nonsense titles like the one I quoted above.

Or, they publish nothing that relates to us at all. I've done extensive searches online, looking for anything in the media that considers our situation from a sympathetic point of view. And in essence I've found a big fat zero.

We are invisible. Despite being a large and growing demographic, nobody is writing, filming or recording anything about us. There are no books about being grandchild-less (well, until this one!).

And there is also very little academic research. A recent article from ABC News Australia contains this bald quote from Dr. Bronwyn Harman, a researcher from Edith Cowan University – "Little is known about grandchildlessness." Do you find that surprising? Considering the rapidly rising numbers of grandchildless people, and the impact it has on mental health in later life, I have to say that I find it astonishing.

Saga magazine, which caters for retired people, did recently publish one article relevant to our experience. A veteran British broadcaster,

Dame Jenni Murray, described her heartache around not being a grandmother. She is 70 and her two sons are in relationships with career-focused women in their thirties (still some hope for her, then).

In the piece, Jenni talks about being jealous of friends who are grandparents, mentions how difficult it is not to "pester" her sons, and says that though she loves her dogs, they are no substitute for grandchildren. It is a relatable and interesting article.

However, when this was republished in The Daily Mail, comments from readers included the following – "Please don't impose your desires on your children", "You should defo get more dogs or hobbies to fulfil this 'yearning' " (note the quote marks; she can't *really* be yearning), and "Why is this news?"

Meanwhile, Saga magazine publishes endless quantities of articles for people who *are* grandparents. They've even started giving their staff a week off for "grandparent leave" when their grandchildren are born, and allowing them to use the crèche at work!

What about TV, films, radio? There's plenty about grandparents, but virtually nothing about us. The website TV Tropes, which documents common themes in TV shows, suggests that "I Want Grandkids" is a theme (or "trope"). But only when it relates to pushy parents demanding grandchildren.

TV Tropes offers us two particular strains of the "I Want Grandkids" trope, as expressed by demanding parents towards their adult children. These are called "You Have Waited Long Enough" and "Not Wanting Kids Is Weird." But neither of these relates to our own experience. We are *not*, by and large, pushy, nor are we generally trying to guilt-trip our children into procreation.

So, TV? No. Films? Nothing relevant that I can find. Radio? Nope. Nothing for us here, folks.

If the print media are no use to us, and TV, radio and films ignore us, how about going online?

If you open YouTube and type "no grandchildren" into the search bar, you'll find a handful of videos about the following topics –

- People who are estranged from their grandkids.
- People saying "no" to their grandkids.
- 'Adorable' videos of people with their pets, and
- Pastors preaching about the Bible verse, "God has no grandchildren".

And that's it.

Moving on, there's Gransnet.

In case you're not familiar with this website, it bills itself as *"the busiest online community for over 50s. At its heart is a discussion forum where users give each other advice and support."* It's designed for grandparents, and no doubt provides a very useful service to them.

Some of the people who use the site, however, are quite ... what's the word? Challenging, maybe? if you go there and post about your lack of grandchildren, and it's advice you're after, then other posters will dole that out with a great big ladle. Support? Not so much.

Occasionally, some poor innocent woman posts that she has no grandchildren and she's sad about it. She can be sure of a big response. A few people may be sympathetic and relatively kind, but in general the comments will fall into one of these three camps –

- Get a hobby and stop feeling sorry for yourself,
- It's none of your business what your children do, or
- I thought I'd never have grandkids either and now I have six!!

Here are some sample comments, responding to a woman who was depressed at not having grandchildren.

"We had given up on grandchildren but DS married at 40 and produced the grandchildren in short order."

"Look on the bright side. There are no little kids to worry about, no terrible anxiety when they're poorly. Your life is unhindered by fitting in with or anticipating their needs etc. etc. - be grateful for your freedom!"

"Do any of your friends have grandchildren you could "share" an interest in? Any young neighbours with no family nearby who might appreciate your friendship? Schools that might welcome a volunteer to listen to the children read?"

"How can you have a loss when you haven't had it in the first instance? Get over it and enjoy your life."

"Don't give up hope - my son was 50 when he started his family now they have two lovely girls!"

"As for the grandchildren, that's their decision and you can't live your life through them. Time to stop fretting about it and get on with your lives."

"I would recommend being a Home Start volunteer. You are a regular visitor and help a family with at least one child under 5 yrs."

"It's not a loss as such if you have never had grandchildren, so there should not be a hole."

And at least this one is honest – "I do not know what to suggest."

Where is the empathy? The original poster has no grandchildren, and minds this terribly. She is hurting badly.

And other women, who are in the lucky and privileged position of having grandchildren, belittle her. They dismiss her pain, they boast about their own grandchildren, they offer "solutions" (do they really think the original poster hasn't thought of those ideas already?) and they tell her in effect to "get a grip".

It's cruel and completely unnecessary, in my view. And my advice to women in our situation, who feel in need of support and validation, is this. Please, don't post about it on Gransnet if you value your mental health.

So there we have it. Generally speaking, the media are not interested in us, other than as objects of pity. If you look for empathic articles about us, positive depictions of older people without grandchildren, or academic research on grandchildlessness, you are likely to come up empty-handed.

That's in large part why I've written this book. It's a start. It says "We exist and we deserve to be recognised and heard."

I hope many more of us come forward and share our stories, when the time comes that we feel safe to do so!

References

"No Grandkids? No Problem!" by Dori Gillam, 3rd Act Magazine, Fall 2018 The Generation Who Won't Be Grandparents, by Briana Shepherd, ABC News Australia, September 21st 2019

SAGA magazine article by Dame Jenni Murray, December 2020 issue, referenced by Sam Baker in The Daily Mail, December 1st 2019

www.tvtropes.org

www.gransnet.com

CHAPTER SIX

MENTAL IMPACT

Disclaimer – What follows is not medical advice. Although I have worked as a counsellor and I'm certified in that field, I have no medical qualifications. I am not a doctor, psychiatrist or clinical psychologist.

If you are struggling significantly with your mood or emotions, and it's impacting your daily life, then you need to speak to your doctor. They should be able to help you.

For many of us, the biggest challenge set by not becoming a grandparent is coping with our feelings. We may experience sadness, envy, frustration, loneliness, anxiety and grief – and more. At various times and with varying intensities, these feelings can colour our everyday lives and make it hard to move forward in a constructive way.

I've left this chapter to the end of Part One, but not because our emotions aren't important. I believe that this element of the book is highly significant. But for many of us it's a challenge to think about, and face up to, our feelings.

So, as I was putting the book together it made sense to look first at the more objective aspects of our grandchildlessness. Why has it happened, how has it changed our lives, what other people think about us, and so on.

Now it's time to talk about emotions.

Traditional models of counselling and psychotherapy tell us that there are four main emotions. These are - Happiness, Sadness, Anger and Fear. If you're from the USA you may know these as Glad, Sad, Mad and Scared. All other feelings are a version of one or more of these four. In reality it's more complicated than that, but it'll do as a starting point.

Obviously, we can rule out happiness as a source of our distress. (My small son once asked me why there were three horrible feelings and only one nice one. It's an interesting question!). We're left with sadness, anger and fear.

Sadness is likely to be the most significant emotion many of us experience in relation to not becoming grandparents. So let's tackle that one first.

Sadness

We are all familiar with sadness. The low mood, the misery, that ache that won't go away. You might find yourself crying frequently, and wonder if the tears will ever stop coming.

There can be other physical symptoms associated with sadness in addition to crying. For example, you might feel it as a heaviness on your chest, or a churning stomach. This is all normal.

Sadness can be a persistent feeling, unfortunately. We can live with it for extended periods, experiencing that downward shift in mood whenever we are reminded of our grandchildlessness.

You're probably familiar with that rush of emotion when you unexpectedly get notified of a friend's daughter's pregnancy, or catch sight of grandparents with a toddler when you're out on a walk. The tears fill your eyes in an instant and a sense of hopelessness sets in.

Although it might not seem like it, sadness is useful. It signals to us that something is missing in our lives. And once we've fully experienced the sadness over that missing thing, we have the opportunity to move forward, finding alternative sources of meaning and pleasure.

The trigger for sadness is often a loss of some sort – a friend moves to another country, our youth and beauty are slipping away, or we've experienced rejection from someone we care about. Some of these are one-off events, and some are ongoing and can take years to fully experience.

We can also be sad about the loss of our hopes and dreams. This is obviously the case with grandchildlessness. And this, by the way, is the answer to anyone who is cruel enough to say "You've never had grandchildren, so how can you be experiencing a loss?"

Our picture of ourselves in the future, surrounded by the grandchildren who give our lives purpose and structure, has been destroyed. Instead we imagine a lonely and meaningless old age ahead (and now, here comes **fear** as well – more on that later.)

It doesn't have to be this way. We will find constructive routes out of this state in Part Two.

Next, I want to look at the difference between sadness and depression.

Depression has been described as "toxic sadness". While we can go on reasonably well with our lives when we're sad, depression tends to disrupt our normal functioning - sometimes to the point where we can no longer cope.

One way to distinguish between sadness and depression is through noticing our physical symptoms. Here are some possible physical indicators of depression -

- you sleep far too much, *or* you have significant insomnia
- you've lost your appetite, eat very little and are losing weight, *or* you can't stop eating
- you're exhausted all the time
- you have unexplained aches and pains, or headaches

Other symptoms are psychological, to do with your mood or thinking.

- you feel low all the time, for a prolonged period
- you're struggling with feelings of hopelessness or guilt
- you can't make decisions
- you've lost interest in your work, hobbies and activities
- you're irritable and snap at people
- you don't want to socialise or leave the house

If you recognise yourself in these lists of symptoms, please go to see your doctor and tell him or her how you're feeling. Untreated depression not only spoils your life, it can be dangerous. Your doctor can help.

You might well benefit from counselling or psychotherapy, or from antidepressant medication, or both. Support is available – please reach out and get it.

Grief

Grief is also related to sadness. We are familiar with the idea of grief that follows the death of a loved one, and many of us will have been through this.

We can also experience grief over the loss of our dreams for the future. *This is real.* Don't let anyone tell you "There never was a grandchild so you can't be grieving." You can.

Some of the physical and mental manifestations of grief can be similar to those of depression. You might also experience a feeling of intense longing. Some people imagine the grandchildren they would have had, and think about what their lives would have been like with these little ones around. This kind of fantasy can seem comforting, but if it goes on for too long it can bring problems of its own.

You may be familiar with the commonest model of grieving, which suggests that we go through five stages – denial, anger, bargaining, depression and acceptance. A structure like this can be useful when we're analysing our situation. We'll look at this model in more detail in Part 2.

Anger

Now we come on to some feelings that might surprise you. Why would anyone feel angry about not having grandchildren?

Well, we might feel angry with life itself, or with fate, for treating us so unfairly. There are plenty of people with grandchildren our there, and some of them are lousy grandparents, too. Why are we being punished like this? Have we done something so wrong - are we cursed?

We might also feel angry with our children for not giving us grandchildren. We were good parents, we did everything by the book and made sacrifices for them, and they repay us by not having babies?

Bear in mind here, that we may know perfectly well it's irrational and unreasonable to blame them like this. A few people think they are owed grandchildren, but most of us accept our children's choice when we think about it calmly.

However, that may not be enough to prevent feelings of anger and resentment emerging from time to time. In Part 2 we'll look at ways to stop ourselves damaging our relationships with our children, which we can do if we allow ourselves to express unthinking rage.

But for now, just know that it's perfectly OK and understandable to feel this way. Our feelings don't have to be logical, and quite often they are not!

Fear

Another surprising emotion, perhaps. But there's a number of ways fear can creep into our outlook on life as we struggle to come to terms with no grandchildren.

We might be fearful as we look ahead into our old age. The image of a loving family surrounding us in our dotage is comforting. Being alone at that stage of life can be a scary prospect.

If we're lucky, our children may provide some support for us in the years ahead. But what about that sense of the future unfolding as we gaze on the youngest members of the clan? We are all too aware that after our kids are gone, that's it for the family. The thought can send a chill down our spine.

And then, there's the anxiety (a mild form of fear) that can accompany any social gathering, or even a trip to the hairdresser or the shops. At any time we may have to field the dreaded question -"Have you got grandchildren?" Or as we age it may morph into "How many grandkids do you have?"

We may have worked out a stock response to this, that saves our feelings and minimises the awkwardness - and we'll look at how to do that in Part 2. But still, it's always going to be a reminder of our status as non-grandparents, and we can become scared of those interactions.

This kind of fear can drive us to shut ourselves away from other people, and then we may worry (worrying is another close relative of fear) that we're becoming reclusive. Again, ways to combat this will be in Part 2.

Shame

Shame can be one of the hardest feelings to combat, because we can usually see how irrational it is. Logically, if we're going to feel ashamed about anything, it needs to be something we ourselves have done wrong. And in this case, it's not our choice or decision – so why the sense of shame?

This often has to do with how we are perceived by society in general. Somehow, there's a sense in the air that we *are* responsible for what's happened. "Only the best mothers get promoted to Grandma" according to a bumper sticker. The implication is that if we're not Grandmas, then we've been inadequate parents, somehow. Otherwise *of course* our children would want babies.

For those from a religious background, this unspoken pressure may be even greater. "Grandchildren are a blessing" is a phrase that gets bandied about. So, does that mean that those without grandchildren are not blessed? Are they undeserving, condemned, even cursed?

All of the above is absolutely not true, so please don't internalise those thoughts. It's mindless, unthinking prejudice from unintelligent or careless people. But it's so vague, so much just part of the air we breathe, that it can be hard to combat. We'll work on that in – yes you guessed it – Part 2.

Alienation

Alienation is the sense of being separated from our social group. It's easy to see how that can arise. As our friends and siblings become grandparents, we feel our former closeness to them gradually slipping away.

They are busy with this new phase of their lives, and we are not part of it. They want to spend time with other grandparents now. Our interests diverge, there's less to talk about and less reason to meet up.

When you throw in the pain we experience when we contrast their lives with ours, it's no surprise if we start avoiding them. But it comes at a cost to us. If we're not careful, our social circle will shrink and we may become isolated and lonely.

Envy

The green-eyed monster. Most of us will have experienced envy at some point in our lives, at least mildly. Someone we know gets the promotion at work, the fancy new car, the financial windfall. Lucky them, and why couldn't it have been us, we might think.

But nowadays, we may be experiencing a whole new level of envy. People we know, people who seem just like us, have the thing we want most in the world, while we can only look on. And often, they don't even seem to appreciate how lucky they are. They've taken it for granted that they'll become grandparents - and then it happens for them.

How is this fair? Well, it isn't fair, of course. That phrase our parents used to trot out when we were young, "Life's not fair", has never rung so true.

Powerlessness

This one might hit you most strongly if you're someone who has been used to having a high level of control over what happens to you.

You've been driven and focused in your approach to life. You've gone along, setting goals and then achieving them. So far that style has served you just fine.

And then, all of a sudden you're not in control *at all*. However much you want grandchildren, there is nothing you can do to make it happen. It's completely outside your power to affect the situation, and it's a huge shock.

We will probably all experience a sense of powerlessness in regard to our lack of grandchildren, even if it's much less extreme than the example above. Not being able to *do* something about a difficult situation can make it much harder to bear.

We need to cultivate serenity and acceptance, but my goodness that's difficult. Some ideas in Part 2 will hopefully help us on that path.

So there we have it. A whistle-stop tour of many of the emotions we may experience as a side-effect of our grandchildless state. Perhaps there were some that particularly resonated with you.

You've reached the end of Part One of the book. I hope it's given you food for thought, and I especially hope that you are feeling less alone now.

We've looked at how we got here, how we're doing so far, and how we may be affected mentally and emotionally. In Part Two we will focus on constructive ways forward. How to manage our thoughts and feelings, how to relate to the people we care about, how to get back our emotional strength and resilience, and how to enjoy life once again.

Let's go!

PART TWO

INTRODUCTION TO PART TWO

So, we've surveyed the scene. In Part 1 we looked at -

- How we got here.
- Why our children don't want children or can't have them.
- What this means for our relationships, and
- How others see us.
- We met our friends Diane, Jeff, Trixie and Vanessa, and heard a little of their stories. Perhaps some of what they said resonated with us too.
- Maybe most importantly, we considered the effect all this is having on our mental health and wellbeing.

And now, in Part 2 of this book, we'll take a deep dive into what we can actually do about it all. How to cope day-to-day. How to find meaning and purpose again. How to relate to the people in our lives.

Part 2 also suggests how we can look after ourselves, both physically and mentally. And, what to do with all the stuff we've been saving!

The first part of this book may have felt like a challenging read at times. It's tough to face up to our lack of grandchildren. Sometimes we want to pretend it isn't happening, bury our heads in the sand and wish it all away.

But in this second half, we're finding positive ways forward. There really can be peace, acceptance and joy in our lives once more.

CHAPTER SEVEN - PART ONE

DEALING WITH FEELING

Our motto – *"It's OK to feel your feelings"*
We are now moving into the "personal development" section of the book. From now on, we'll be considering in practical terms what we can actually do to feel happier and lead more meaningful and fulfilling lives, without grandchildren.

In chapter 6, we looked at various psychological states from an "outside" perspective. So, we've been through the definitions and we know the major emotions we're likely to be encountering.

Now it's time to consider what this means for us, personally. What are we actually experiencing, minute by minute, day by day, year by year?

How do *we feel* about not becoming a grandparent?

"Feeling" words can scare us. They're so raw, so real. We can take refuge in thinking instead, and distance ourselves from our own experience. "Well, it's sad of course, but what can you do?" is the kind of calm and logical response to grandchildlessness that we try to adopt. And this can be what we present to the world, too. Inside though, we're destroyed by sadness, anger and grief.

We can distance ourselves by not taking ownership of those feelings. "It's difficult", "Life's not fair", "You just have to get on with things, don't you?".

Instead of this, we are going to start using the pronoun "I". Even doing this can be a challenge for some of us, myself included, who were taught as children that it was boasting to talk about ourselves!!

It is acceptable, fine and admirable to talk about ourselves. Let's use "I" and own our feelings.

Being in touch with what we feel is very important because it's the pathway to beginning healing. That is the end goal here, after all. To reach acceptance and peace with what fate has thrown in our path.

It is OK to experience strong feelings. However, women are often taught, either explicitly or subliminally, that it's not acceptable. We can even be encouraged to suppress them, perhaps by adults (including our parents) who are afraid of strong emotions and don't know how to handle their own, let alone those of a child.

In particular we're not meant to be angry. We might have hoped that this was an outdated view, but just look at the current internet meme about "Karen". She's a satirical representation of an outspoken and angry middle-aged woman, and the butt of endless contemptuous jokes. The message is alive and well in the 21st century. Women, know your place!

Men can suffer from this societal bias too. We do occasionally see men cry these days, but how acceptable is it, really? How OK is it for a man to admit to fear?

Well, my message is different. We *are* allowed to feel more than just sadness about our grandchildlessness (though we'll experience sadness in abundance, of course).

We can be furiously angry, if that's the feeling we're experiencing. We can be scared. We can be envious of others, and that can be one of the strongest of emotions. And so on.

Of course, there is a time and a place to display our emotions. It might not be the best idea to have a complete meltdown in a supermarket or in church if we can help it, for example.

But my point is, it is not just OK, it's healthy to allow ourselves to feel our feelings. They are there for a purpose, and repressing them often leads to serious problems down the line, including depression and various physical ailments.

Above all, we can *grieve*, and this will be a big part of the healing for many of us. It was only when I truly accepted that I was going through grief, that I began to have calmer, more accepting moments. So grief is going to be a major focus here.

Ready for some experience of recognising and naming your feelings?

ACTION POINT - when a feeling arises in you, see if you can name it. Own that feeling – say it, out loud if possible, or at least inside your mind. Or write it down. Go for one of the big three feelings to start with, sadness, anger or fear.

This may be a challenge to you if you've only ever thought in terms of feeling either OK or bad. And that's fine. Many people go through life without thinking deeply about their emotions like this.

If this exercise is too easy, though, try to be more specific in naming the feeling. Phrase it like this – "Right now, I'm feeling furious/miserable/hopeless/jealous" or whichever the emotion is.

How was that experience for you? If you felt anxious or wobbly from saying it out loud, that's completely understandable. You've gone against decades of conditioning and done something very new. Tell yourself "Well done", make sure you're warm, get a cup of tea or coffee or a cool drink.

Notice where in your body you have sensations, when you acknowledge your feelings. Does your stomach churn, do you feel lightheaded, are you catching your breath? Or, any number of other physical manifestations? This is all fine and normal. Again, take care of yourself – as if you were looking after a vulnerable child, if that helps.

More feelings may rise to the surface as you acknowledge the first emotion. That's fine. We are complex beings, and this is a complex situation. Let them come, naming them if you can.

Repeat this exercise over the next days and weeks, if possible. The more practice we have in this the better. Gradually, you may find you get quicker at identifying which feeling it is, partly from the physical sensations. It's all part of acknowledging what we're going through.

Take it gently. If you feel too stressed when you do this exercise, leave it for now. There's no rush. Maybe try again in a few days when the time seems more appropriate. And as always, if you're finding the experience overwhelming or disturbing, then professional counselling support might be the way to go for you.

Now let's consider some of the big emotions; how we experience them and how to handle them. We'll leave grieving to the end, as that's the most complex.

Sadness

Do you find yourself feeling a lot of sadness these days? If so, how does it show itself – a heaviness in your chest, perhaps, lethargy and tiredness, or the commonest of all – crying.

There is nothing inherently wrong with being sad, and it's certainly important to be aware when we are feeling that way. It's an emotion which is normal and the body's natural way of coming to terms with the adverse things that happen to us as we go through our lives.

But it's also quite easy to get into the habit of thinking sad thoughts and lowering our mood unnecessarily. When it becomes a habit, it's no longer therapeutic.

The aim here is to discover ways to stop that happening. Nobody wants to be sad all the time, after all.

Distraction, and moving into being in the moment, both work quite well when we are sad. After all, we're usually dwelling on thoughts or wishes that are nothing to do with the here-and-now. Our bodies can't tell the difference between what we're thinking of, and what's really happening – so tell your body that life is actually OK right at this moment.

Instead of staying with your sad thoughts, put on some music and sing along; recite something you know off by heart (a nursery rhyme or song lyric will do); move, change scenery, watch a favourite TV show or pick up a crossword. Anything of this sort that works for you is fine. And of course, there's always my standard British answer to most things – make a cup of tea (or coffee, if you prefer!)

This may sound a bit like someone telling you to "Just cheer up". But the object is to put yourself in charge of how you are feeling. You're not following someone else's unhelpful advice, you are choosing to behave differently. That can be empowering.

Physical contact often helps to comfort us when we're sad. A hug from a person who cares about us is great. So is cuddling a pet, or even hugging a stuffed toy. (But think twice about asking for support from a child – do you really want to dump your emotional troubles on them?)

These tactics won't change anything about the past or future, of course. But the important thing is, it will change NOW. Because you ARE OK at the moment. And this moment is all we ever actually have. We live right now, not in the past or the future.

Crying is often a worry to people, so let's consider that in more detail. Allowing the tears to fall is usually beneficial, so don't feel you have to make a big effort not to cry. Even massive crying jags are self-limiting. After about twenty minutes, we're usually tired enough that our body naturally stops the tears. So if you're concerned that once you start crying you won't be able to stop, there's no need. You will.

Recent research has demonstrated the physical benefits of crying. Tears contain stress hormones and toxins, so by ridding our bodies of these undesirable materials, we can make ourselves feel physically calmer. Tests have shown that he heart-rate of people who cry at a sad image or film, returns to normal faster than in those who see the same images but don't cry.

So if we can reframe the act of crying as something that's helpful to us, it sheds a whole new light on the situation. We can wipe away those stress hormones with our tears and know that our bodies are healthier for the experience. Few of us really enjoy crying, but this can be an encouraging thought while we're going through it.

As before though, if you find yourself sinking into a phase where you cry frequently (daily, or even several times a day) and don't feel better for it, you may be lapsing into depression and it's a good idea to take medical advice.

ACTION POINT – next time you're sad, try some of the ideas above. Distract yourself, make sure you're warm and comfortable, engage in a task you know you'll enjoy (not chores!) and seek physical reassurance from people, pets or even by wrapping yourself in a duvet. See if it helps you. But, don't stop the tears coming, as they will do you good.

Anger

We may know when we're angry, but alternatively we may have repressed the whole idea of anger for so long that we aren't fully aware of the emotion when it arises.

Physical signs can include a churning stomach, feeling hot and/or sweaty, clenching your teeth or fists, feeling shaky and noticing your heart beating.

Alternatively, some people (especially women) may find themselves crying when they are angry. This is sometimes known in psychotherapy as a "racket emotion". It's when we allow ourselves to feel one socially acceptable feeling in place of another, more problematic one. All completely unconscious of course!

So in this case, the inappropriate (but socially sanctioned) feeling of sadness masks the authentic emotion, anger. I'm talking about this here because it's often quite confusing to people when it happens. I've heard a woman say, "I don't know why I'm crying; really I'm very angry!".

Anger is a perfectly reasonable emotion to feel in response to our lack of grandchildren. We can easily feel angry with fate for dealing us this lousy hand. Plenty of people who have been terrible parents get to have grandkids, after all, so why not us, when we worked so hard at raising our children?

This is demonstrably true, and as long as we don't get stuck in a cycle of dwelling on thoughts like this I don't think there's a problem here. It IS unfair, no two ways about it. Let's acknowledge that fact, deal with our anger (more on how to do this below) and move on.

We might also feel angry with ourselves, for example for not having more babies and increasing our chances. Or, we can feel angry with our children – they've let us down, or they are selfish and ungrateful.

Here we're skating on thinner ice. Blame is seldom useful. We can end up punishing ourselves or berating our children and these kinds of actions are definitely not helpful or constructive.

Here are some more useful ideas for what to do when you feel angry -

---

ACTION POINT – Anger can be a very energizing emotion, and one way to put it to good use is to channel that energy into a physical task. Dig the garden, go for a vigorous walk, blitz through the housework or put on some music and dance till you're dizzy.

Alternatively, let out the rage as well as the energy by pummelling a pillow or yelling yourself hoarse (pick a suitable place and time for the latter, obviously.) Once the storm is past you're likely to find yourself feeling tired, but much calmer. That's good!

Don't be afraid of anger. It has its place in the healing process, and like every other emotion it is self-limiting. Just try your very best not to take out your fury on other people, or indeed on yourself. We'll be looking at how to talk to our nearest and dearest later.

Envy

"Comparison is the thief of joy" as the old saying has it.

It's very common to compare ourselves to others. In fact, we've probably been coached in this activity from an early age. For example, I had an older cousin who was held up as a paragon of every virtue. A frequent refrain from my mother throughout my childhood was "Why can't you be more like Hannah?" Not kind, and not useful!

We may have felt ourselves to be quite fortunate in our lives up to now. For one thing, we've been able to have children, and we're well aware of the pain of people who long for their own family but are cursed with infertility.

And from our new, enlightened position as grandchildless older adults, we may even wonder if we've been insensitive in the past, in the same way that we're finding our peers who are grandparents insensitive towards us. Did we talk about our children too much? Did we forget that some of our friends weren't also in the happy position of tired but proud parents of infants? Did we hurt them, the way we're being hurt now?

In any case, these days boot is well and truly on the other foot. We are only too aware that grandparents can be inconsiderate!

There seems to be something about becoming a grandparent that drives apparently rational people slightly crazy. You would think ordinary tact and kindness would prevent our friends and relatives who have grandkids from endlessly talking about it and rubbing our noses in their good fortune. They are supposed to care about us, after all.

But you'd be wrong. It doesn't seem to cross their minds for a moment to hold their tongues. They bombard us with stories and images of their (perfectly ordinary) grandchildren at every opportunity.

It's seen as a "safe" topic of conversation. Who could possibly be offended by them talking about their wonderful grandkids?

It's not surprising that we feel aggrieved. It's hurtful and upsetting. And naturally, it can trigger intense feelings of envy; that painful longing to have what someone else has, and resentment of them for having it when we don't.

Dealing with these feelings can be tricky. Point number one is not to feel bad about experiencing envy. It's natural and normal. You don't deserve to beat yourself up over an emotion you think you "shouldn't" be experiencing, so give yourself a break. You're human!

Practically speaking, there is nothing wrong with minimising the occasions that may trigger your envy. You do NOT have to go to every baby shower, christening, or toddler birthday party, even if these involve your sister's or best friend's grandkids. If you are on social media and get sick of the photos and memes, stop looking at them. Either take a break from the platform, or snooze the person who's upsetting you.

If you have friendships or family members that don't involve grandchildren, cherish them. As always, distractions help – new activities or hobbies in particular.

My next point may feel challenging, but bear with me. We need to be grateful for what we do have. "I'd swap all of that for just one grandchild," you may be thinking. But would you, really? It's so easy to take our good fortune for granted. If we have a loving relationship with our spouse or partner, for example, it's a blessing that many would envy us for. If we're decently housed, have enough to eat, are warm and comfortable, we are lucky compared to many other people in the world.

And maybe we have other things that people envy us for. Talent, for example, which covers a huge number of topics. An attractive personality. A successful career. Good looks, money, supportive people around us, "successful" children, a lovely garden, the ability to travel, a nice house, a collection of something – the list goes on. Any one of these things can be envy triggers for other people, yet we may barely have considered that as a possibility.

In other words, it helps to take a wider view. In addition, some of those people with grandchildren are going to be struggling in other ways. They might have health issues, family relationship difficulties or money worries. All we see is the grandkids (and even those children might have problems we're not aware of).

I know this doesn't solve the problem. But if we think of our lives as a pair of scales, with good fortune on one side and bad on the other, an appreciation of the better things in our lives can help to redress the balance.

ACTION POINT – Practise self-care by minimising contact with people who trigger envious feelings. Seek our people and activities that don't trigger those feelings. Be grateful for what is good in your life and remember we can't see below the surface of others' lives.

Embarrassment and Shame

These two emotions are closely linked, but the simple way to tell them apart is that embarrassment tends to occur in social situations, while shame is more of an internal feeling. Shame can occur when we feel we've done something wrong. Embarrassment is usually accompanied by a feeling of being exposed when we have somehow transgressed social norms.

You may experience one or both of these since they are both common feelings in response to our grandchildless situation.

Let's consider embarrassment first. How do you feel when someone asks you if you have grandchildren? Are you unsure how to reply? Do you anticipate an uncomfortable or awkward moment when you tell them you don't? Perhaps you're aware of your heart beating faster, or you may blush or stammer.

Of course, this question digs away at a sore spot inside us. Yet again we're being forced to confront the painful truth. But the embarrassment itself arises mainly from the knowledge that we are about to tell the other person something they don't expect to hear – something that will cause a socially difficult moment for them as well as for us. We can find ourselves wishing we were somewhere else and not having to go through this, and the repetition of such experiences can even lead us to withdraw from events where we're likely to get triggered in this way.

In Chapter 8, How to talk to people, we'll look at ways to avoid at least some of this embarrassment by working out standard responses to difficult questions. For now though, we can acknowledge that embarrassment is a normal response to a situation where we know we fall outside what's expected of us.

However, it *is* possible to grow a thicker skin. We can at least remind ourselves that it just doesn't matter what a complete stranger, or someone we met at a party, thinks of us! We'll probably never see them again, so who cares?

Hang on to this thought till we get to the next chapter.

Shame can be a more troubling emotion to experience. We might feel that we've somehow failed to live up to the standards we expected of ourselves, or we've disappointed people who are important to us. Even though in reality we have no responsibility for our lack of grandchildren, we might feel deep down that we do.

Do you sometimes wonder if you did something wrong and that's what has caused you not to have grandchildren? That you're being punished, or you were a bad mother? We may feel devalued or even guilty. These thoughts and feelings can lead into an overall sense of shame.

We can call on our rational self here to help us out. It will tell us that we were good enough parents, and that's all we can ask of ourselves. It'll also point out that really terrible parents frequently become grandparents.

In fact, the better-educated someone is, the less likely they are to have children. And socially-aware young people, the kind who reject procreation because of their perception that it's bad for the planet, are usually intelligent, sensitive types who think deeply about the world.

These individuals are not the product of bad parenting, surely? You did a fine job if you've raised a child like this. The fact that they don't want, or can't have, a baby is a terrible misfortune from our point of view, but it is not due to bad parenting and it is **not our fault**.

And no, you are NOT being punished for something you did in the past. We can agonise over a past indiscretion or difficult decision. Our divorce, for example, or that time we went away because of work and missed a vital moment in our child's life. Or even much more minor events that still prey on our minds.

These things do not cause grandchildlessness.

Stay in touch with reality. Much of what happens is quite random, and that can be difficult to understand if life has treated us pretty well up to now. We are often not responsible for our good fortune, though we may think we've deserved it. So equally, we've not earned the bad luck that's come our way now.

ACTION POINT – Accept that it's normal to feel embarrassed or ashamed because of grandchildlessness. Then harness your logical side to remind yourself that it really doesn't matter much what people think, and that you've done nothing wrong.

Dealing with feelings is often the most challenging part of this journey. It may help to revisit this chapter every so often and consider how far you've come in understanding and coping with difficult emotions. If you feel very stuck, you may benefit from professional help such as seeing a counsellor for a while.

Do what you can, treat yourself with gentle compassion, and hopefully you will gradually find the pain eases and your sense of peace and acceptance grows.

GRIEF

Our motto – *"First there is loss. Then there is grief, and finally there is recreating our lives."*

If there's one thing people say to us about our grandchildless state that grinds my gears more than any other, it's this - "You can't miss what you never had." Or other words to that effect. Have you heard this kind of thing? "You haven't lost anything because you never were a grandparent," "I don't know what you're so sad about," "Stacey's grandson died, so she *really* has a reason to grieve."

As if our dreams, hopes and longings are nothing, and don't count. As if we're not entitled to our pain, somehow.

Well, we *are* entitled to it. Grief encompasses a wide range of different kinds of loss, not just the death of someone who was close to us. If you've experienced that kind of grief (and many of us have by this stage of our lives) then you'll know the intense anguish that can be involved and also the way in which the pain of grief can seem to come and go in waves. You may already be familiar with those five stages of grief that people talk about – disbelief, anger, bargaining, depression and eventually, acceptance.

The grief of grandchildlessness may be a little different, in that it can take many years for us to finally realise we won't be grandparents. So it can be a prolonged process, and that may mean we miss the most acute phases that characterise "normal" grief. It can also mean that we don't identify what we're going through as grief at all.

But it is still grief, because it's about significant losses, and how or if we are able to accept them. The loss of the role of grandparent. The loss of our vision of the future. The loss of status. The loss of our family line. The loss of the structure and activity we looked forward to later in life. The loss of a new closeness with our adult children as they experience parenthood. The loss of the loving relationships we could have had with the grandchildren who will never exist.

It's no wonder we're grieving, and one risk with this kind of long-drawn-out process is that we can become stuck for years in sadness and low-grade depression.

Here are some of the normal symptoms of grief, both physical and psychological -

Physical – as well as crying, there are many other possible symptoms. Loss of appetite, weight loss, digestive upset, nausea, insomnia, fatigue, low energy levels, muscle weakness, shakiness, worsened allergies. This is not a complete list, and it's now also thought that the physical impact of grief causes an inflammatory response in the body, which can trigger a multitude of undesirable outcomes.

Psychological – sadness, low mood and depression are symptoms we would all expect. Other possibilities include anxiety and panic attacks, alcohol and drug abuse (this can include prescription drugs), phobias and post-traumatic stress disorder.

Specific mood disorders include irritability and anger, bitterness, hopelessness, a numb feeling, preoccupation with the loss (not being able to think about anything else), a sense of detachment from the world, and anhedonia, which is an inability to experience pleasure or joy.

It's quite a list, isn't it. You may well recognise some of these as applying to you. Don't panic - remember, these are normal reactions, and generally self-limiting. And, we're going to look at ways of coping and getting past them.

Since the realisation that we won't have grandchildren is often a slow process, the more acute problems listed above are less likely to happen. Nevertheless, it's easy to slip into bad habits. For example, drinking too much alcohol can creep up on us without our really being aware of it.

Our phobias might worsen, leading to restrictions in the ways we lead our lives, and we may not be aware of the link to our grief. We may find that chronic insomnia or poor appetite become normal for us, and again, not make the connection to our experience of loss. And so on.

ACTION POINT – get a pen and some paper. Go through the symptoms outlined above, and write down any that apply to you. Then reflect on the extent to which they may be linked to your grandchildlessness. You probably won't be able to tell for sure, of course, but consider that there might be such a connection.

Now think about how long you've been experiencing these feelings and physical symptoms.

If it's under a year, your recognition of your grandchildless situation will be probably fairly recent, and it's very normal to be experiencing strong emotions. The comments in Chapter 7 part 1, especially those focussing on sadness and anger, are likely to be highly relevant to you. You might find you have phases of feeling relatively OK and then days or weeks when it's much harder to cope. This is a common experience.

If however it's been more than a year, consider whether your "symptoms" – that is, your feelings as well as the physical manifestations - have changed. Perhaps they've become less intense, for example, or intermittent rather than constant. That may give you some measure of how far you've come through the grieving process already.

The Five Stages of Grief

Remember the model with the five stages of grieving? You can measure your progress using that. It's important to know that the five stages can overlap, and you might occasionally regress from one stage to a previous one or even skip a stage altogether.

Also, there are other models of grief – the "Five Stages" is just one way to look at our experience. But it still provides a useful rough guide, and it's widely used and understood, so this is the model we'll adopt.

Stage 1 - Disbelief

So, where would you say you are with your grief journey? If you still have difficulty believing it's happening to you, that may indicate you're near the beginning, in Stage 1 – disbelief. Perhaps you just can't believe that your child won't change their mind, or that all your hopes and dreams are for nothing. You might feel as if you're in a dream and will wake up soon. That incredulous feeling can come and go for a long time.

Stage 2 - Anger

As we've seen, you might be angry with your child, or with fate itself. You may rant (to yourself, or perhaps to others) about how unfair it is. Seeing grandparents with their grandkids, or hearing news about an impending grandchild, might leave you feeling enraged rather than sad.

Stage 3 - Bargaining

This is a catch-all term, which might cover attempts on your part to persuade your child to have a baby after all, if they are able. You might (unwisely) try bribery, or even threats such as cutting them out of your will if they don't reproduce.

This can be a dangerous time for family relationships. See the next chapter for ideas on how to talk to your child, but bear in mind that your pleas or threats are very likely to fall on deaf ears, and may also cause great harm to the relationship, including estrangement in extreme cases. Beware!

This stage is also thought of in terms of bargaining with God. People may pray for a grandchild. They might promise to be good, to give up various bad habits, to devote themselves to serving others – if only they can have that grandchild after all.

Stage 4 – Depression

This is probably what we are most familiar with and what comes to mind first when we think of grief. Sadness, crying and a low mood are very common as we allow the reality of what's happened to sink in. This phase can be persistent, or it can come and go over a long period of time. However, it is the first of the "reality" stages, where we are no longer trying to escape from what's happening, but instead facing the painful truth.

Stage 5 – Acceptance

Gradually, as time passes, the feelings may become less acute and we can find that our sense of loss is not occupying our thoughts to the same overwhelming extent as before. We begin to resume our interest in other aspects of our lives, and even start looking forward to new things. Again, this may well be a stage that comes and goes, and there will still be dark days. But we are on our way to a life of acceptance, having on the whole made our peace with what has happened. Life goes on, and we move on with it.

Getting stuck in grieving

If you feel that your experience of grieving has been much the same for a long time, you may be stuck in *prolonged grief*. Using the five stages, you might be able to identify a particular point where you've come to rest and stopped making progress. In that case, it's possible that you need some professional support to help you through. Prolonged grief is characterised by a sense of being trapped by grief; not wanting to accept the finality of the loss; numbness, and/or bitterness; hopelessness when you contemplate the future, and a feeling there's nothing to look forward to and no point in anything.

This is clearly a very dark place to be. If this sounds like you then I would urge you to go and see your doctor, and tell them honestly how you feel. Even if they don't understand how your grief is linked to your lack of grandchildren, they should take your symptoms seriously and provide support, which may be grief counselling, medication or both.

***

Grief is a difficult, painful and sometimes frightening experience. You need to be kind to yourself while going through it, and do your best to ignore any unhelpful or ignorant comments that may come your way.

Even if you know nobody in real life who is in the same situation, at least you know from reading this book that it's a valid and not uncommon experience. There are many others out in the world who also have no grandchildren, and who are suffering just as you are.

Take comfort from that thought. Others have come through this and moved on to a happier and more fulfilling life.

You can too.

HOW TO TALK TO PEOPLE ABOUT GRANDCHILDLESSNESS

Our motto – *"Communication works if we work at it."*

Taboo subjects. There aren't that many of them these days, are there?

It used to be considered bad manners to talk about all sorts of topics. "Don't discuss money or politics at the dinner table" is one old saying I remember from my childhood. And mentioning death was right out.

Anything to do with sex was completely unacceptable too. I must have known some gay people when I was growing up, for example, but it was never acknowledged.

Women who were obviously pregnant were a bit embarrassing, and the menopause was a real trial for those who were going through it and had to pretend nothing was happening. These days women talk openly about menopause, including on TV and other media, and politicians campaign for greater rights for menopausal women in the workplace. That's tremendous progress, but also an astonishing change from how things used to be.

Illness in general wasn't discussed much, and I have to admit that here, I sometimes long for those days. One particularly dreary aspect of getting older is having to listen to contemporaries droning on about their latest source of pain or their recent operation. It's not that I don't sympathise, but it's not much fun for the listener!

My point is, nowadays all of these topics are pretty much out in the open. Even involuntary childlessness is discussed, though those who are sadly experiencing it may well feel that it still isn't as socially accepted as it should be.

But while most intelligent people have, mercifully, learned not to say "pull yourself together" to someone who is depressed, there isn't always that kind of compassion for us. In fact, people can be thoughtless, unkind and intolerant, and an experience of this kind of response can make it hard for us to trust or open up again in the future.

So, where are we with telling people about our grandchildless lives? Have we met with kindness and respect if we want to talk about our sadness, disappointment or sense of loss? Or the opposite?

Let's look at a couple of examples that did not work out well.

Talking to friends and family

Here is what happened to Vanessa.

"I felt the need to talk about how low I was feeling as a result of knowing I'd never be a Grandma. I was having lunch with two of my oldest friends, who are both grandmothers and were chatting to each other about that. I kind of blurted out how miserable my situation was making me.

They laughed at me. They stared at me and then glanced at each other, and then they actually laughed. Then they became aware of how bad that looked, and they got all flushed and awkward. It was horrible."

Vanessa's friends did not know how to react. They were deeply uncomfortable with what she was saying, and couldn't summon up an appropriate response. She was left feeling ashamed and excluded.

The message she got, loud and clear, was that she shouldn't have said anything. Her friends did not want to hear it and she made them deeply uncomfortable by bringing the topic up.

Trixie had this experience.

> *"My cousin had her first grandchild, a little boy. She sent me endless pictures of him, and reported his progress in minute detail.*
>
> *A couple of times I mentioned that it was sad for me not having a grandchild, hoping she'd take a hint and back off. Instead she redoubled the sending of the photos! Maybe she thought she was cheering me up.*
>
> *In the end I asked her nicely not to send so much, as it upset me. She stopped completely. I didn't hear from her for several months, despite me sending her occasional friendly messages.*
>
> *We are back in touch now, but I don't feel we are as close as before. It's like I just can't win."*

Trixie's cousin presumably believed that everyone loves a baby, and so it was fine to bombard her cousin with these baby photos. She was blind to Trixie's pain. When she couldn't avoid the truth any more, she chose to be offended, as if Trixie had transgressed against some unspoken code.

The message Trixie got was that she shouldn't have raised the subject. She was expected to endure her cousin's insensitive boasting and not say a word about it. And when she broke this "rule", she was punished in traditional fashion via the silent treatment.

We are back to the words that opened this chapter. Talking about our pain as grandchildless people is taboo. That's extraordinary in a world where naked people appear on TV and swearing is commonplace everywhere. But it seems to be absolutely true.

Here's where I think some of the difficulty may lie -

Firstly, this is an unsolvable problem. Many people like to jump in with a solution to someone else's pain, rather than just accepting it and being there for us, which is what we need. They are made deeply uncomfortable by an issue for which there's no cure.

Involuntarily childless people suffer a lot from this. "You could always adopt," or "Just keep trying, you never know" are the sort of crass responses they hear all too often.

And for us, there isn't even this kind of response available. We can't adopt a grandchild and we can't keep trying.

Secondly, people assume that we think our children owe us grandchildren. They believe we're being selfish.

As a result they may say things like, "That's up to your daughter, isn't it?" Or "You can't make them have children, it's their life".

Yes, we understand that. Few of us sincerely believe that we are "owed" grandchildren, and while we might sometimes have mentioned our sadness to our children, we try not to harp on about it. (There will be more about this below, since talking to our children about the subject is important, difficult and fraught with risk.)

But at the same time, we *are* sad, bitterly disappointed and often depressed. We are grieving. We *do* feel left out and isolated, consigned to the margins of family life when we hoped still to be a vital part of it.

In other words, two things are true at the same time. While we respect our children's autonomy, the decision it has led them to causes great distress for us. We are sad as a result of a choice that makes them happy.

And if the reason for our grandchildlessness is that our son or daughter *can't* have children, then this casual assumption that we're being selfish is even more painful.

What can we do, then, if we need to talk but so few people are willing to listen?

Well, we can try to find others in our situation. If you have grandchildless friends, treasure them. Always bear in mind, though, that if they have children they might yet become grandparents. People who do not have children but are around our age can be a great source of new friendships.

We can keep a journal, and write down our distress. This can also become a record of our journey towards acceptance and peace. Putting the words on paper or a computer screen can help to stop them swirling around in our heads and causing us to suffer.

There are other ways to release our feelings via a creative activity. Those of us who are artistic or musical may find expression through our use of those media, for example.

It may help to talk to a counsellor. The relief of being able to blurt out all our pain and distress once a week, to someone who won't judge us and who is able to just listen, can be enormous. We can feel lighter, more able to cope.

Don't let yourself hold back from counselling by any sense of it not being for "people like me". It is for anyone who needs to talk in a safe and supportive environment.

You may benefit most from a gentle, person centred approach rather than anything that focuses too much on problem-solving, though. So if you go down this route, choose your counsellor carefully and remember you can always change to a different one if you need to.

Talking to our children

This is very important. The way we approach talking to our children about all of this, has the potential to affect our relationship with them for years to come.

We can cause great harm and even estrangement if we get it wrong, and some people have done just that. So we really, really need to think before we speak.

As I see it, we have two main options. One is to talk about grandchildlessness with them, and the other is not to. So the first decision is which of these paths to choose.

And something to consider straight away, is that you *do* have a choice here. You are not obliged to tell them. You might feel somehow that you "have" to talk about it but you really don't.

Remember that you can always talk to someone else, if you need to express your grief or relieve your feelings. It never *has* to be your children who hear this.

It can be very helpful to look at this from your child's point of view, as best you can. How will they feel about you telling them? Will they feel judged, or blamed? Do they think it's basically your problem, not theirs?

Also bear in mind that they are adults, like you, and can raise the subject themselves if they want to. If they're concerned about your mental state for example, and ask you what's wrong, then this might be a good time to tell them. You still need to be careful though, so think about using the ideas in the section below.

It is up to you to make the decision.

If you've already broached the subject then of course your situation is different, and we'll look at that a bit later on.

Not discussing "no grandchildren" with our children.

It may help to consider the pros and cons of this approach.

Pros

We can't hurt or alienate them. They cannot misunderstand us. We don't run the risk of damaging our relationship, at least not because of a major row or a rift. We are showing respect for their decisions and an understanding that it's our problem, not theirs.

Cons

We might consider this such an important part of our lives that we need to share it with them, or we think they need to know. We may feel they already know something is wrong. We can believe that our close relationship with our children will be damaged if they don't understand our position.

You can see straight away the fundamental difference here. If we don't talk about it with them, we won't do various kinds of damage. If we do, we may or may not cause that damage. On the other hand, we might end up closer together because they understand us better.

So, what kind of relationship do you currently have? Do you discuss things like mental health and relationships with them, or they with you? Or is it a more distant, but still loving relationship where you are there for each other, but have distinct areas that are not up for discussion?

If it's the former, that might be the kind of set-up where you could bring up the topic, since you're already used to talking about feelings. If it's a more distant relationship, there may be more of an upset if you start talking about it.

And if you have a difficult or remote relationship already with a son or daughter, consider if it could possibly help to tell them you're sad because they don't have kids. Or, would it be better to work on repairing your connection before you even think about going there?

The old adage "Least said, soonest mended" may be your watchword if you decide that not talking about it with them is the best path for you.

And you might want to consider this. If you have already lost the chance for grandchildren, then your children are more precious than ever. You will need them as you get older.

Not telling them how we feel about not being grandparents is the default position. It's safest. You can always change your mind, but once you've opened the subject up you can never go back and unsay it.

However, some of you will have decided you want to go there, or you may already have done so. Let's consider how that might work.

Choosing to discuss "no grandchildren" with our children

These are my suggestions. Naturally, it's up to you how you choose to do this, but you may want to at least consider these ideas. They may give you some structure or pointers when you're choosing how to approach the subject.

By the way, I intend these pointers mainly for those of us whose child or children have *chosen* not to become parents. It will be a different conversation if your child is involuntarily childless, and if that's the case then I suggest that you proceed even more gently and compassionately.

Remember that **your message is twofold**. One, **we respect their decision not to have children**. Two, **we are sad about not becoming grandparents.** These two things are both true at the same time. That can be hard for anyone to wrap their head around, so don't be surprised if it takes them a while to grasp what you are telling them.

OK, here we go.

Be very clear in your own mind what you're going to say. But equally, be aware that the conversation may get side tracked or even derailed entirely. Get ready to encounter questions, denials and even outright hostility from your children.

Be in a good place yourself, mentally and physically. Don't do this if you are unwell, unduly tired, or stressed out.

If you have more than one child, tell both or all of them together. It's not helpful to talk to one, and then have them tell their sibling, who will feel excluded and probably resentful.

You could combine this with a structured family event like a dinner or barbecue, but preferably not at a restaurant or any other place where people may feel like they can't leave if they want to without causing a scene.

Don't drink heavily, before or during the event.

Make sure it's easy to provide comfort for those involved. Lay on (non-alcoholic) drinks, food, tissues and throws or blankets. Upset people can be soothed by these kinds of physical reassurances.

Don't insist that people continue, or even stay, if it goes badly.

Try to listen at least as much as you speak.

As you probably gather from all this, I suggest a one-time event where you calmly explain how you're feeling about not having grandchildren and how it's affecting you mentally and emotionally. Once you've said it there is little reason to say it again, ever. They won't forget!

Ask them what they think. Be open to them, and do everything you can to listen to what they say without judgement. They may be accepting and kind, but equally they may be angry or hurt and lash out. Try to stay calm regardless.

Do not blame your children. You must emphasis that you respect their right to choose. If, deep down, you *do* blame them then I suggest

GUIDE TO NO GRANDCHILDREN

working on that before you take this step. It really is their life, their body and their choice. That's tough on us, but we need to come to terms with the reality here.

Whatever you do, don't let this escalate into a slanging match or blame game. If you feel it's going badly then it's fine to call time. But don't grimly inform them that it's not over and they'll have to hear it all again later. They are entitled not to listen to you, if that's their choice.

I've made this sound very difficult, and I do think it's full of potential pitfalls. But, I do also believe it can work. Good luck if you choose this path!

Next, here are a few things *not to do*.

» Don't nag, hint or whine.

As I said, this should be a one-time event. If you find yourself dropping hints about grandchildren, or sighing over pictures of babies when your children are around, or talking about their cousin who is pregnant, then stop. It's either annoying or hurtful to your child, quite probably both, and it's not good for your relationship with them.

We might tell ourselves that we "hardly ever" mention the subject, but our child may feel we talk about it almost continuously if we indulge in this kind of low-grade complaining. If you've got into the habit of doing this kind of thing, then make a concerted effort to notice when it happens and stop yourself.

By all means talk to a sympathetic friend, your journal or your counsellor about it all. Just not your kid.

» Don't bribe or threaten.

"If you have a baby, I will ..... look after it so you can go back to work, pay for all your holidays, fund the child's education, leave you the house in my will."

"If you don't have a baby, I will .... take back that thing I gave you, stop hosting that event we have every year, cut you off financially, never speak to you again."

Doesn't all of that sound awful? If you're very upset, it might be tempting to say something like this.

Don't go there.

» Don't try to change their mind.

You daughter or son has come to a decision not to have children. This is unlikely to be a whim, unless they are still very young. Once they reach their mid-twenties, say, they have probably thought seriously about whether or not they want babies. If they are willing to tell you that you are not going to be a grandparent, knowing how disappointed you'll be, then they mean what they say.

So it follows that you can't persuade them or reason them out of their decision, and any attempt to do that is likely to backfire. The last thing you want is to push them into an ever firmer decision!

Remember too that the reason they give you for not wanting kids might not be complete, or even accurate.

For example, they might say children are too expensive. And you might think, "Aha! All I have to do is offer to pay for various things. Problem solved!" Then you may feel mystified when they *still* don't want a baby.

Probably though, they just reached for an excuse they thought would satisfy you. They may have multiple reasons, or one they don't want to tell you. It's their business, and we delve into their psyche at our peril.

And remember, *it is always their choice*. Having a child is a massive commitment. If they don't want that, for whatever reason, what do you think you could possibly say that would make a difference? It's not as if we can have a baby for them.

We may have to bite our tongue. And that may be very hard for us, believing as we do that they are missing out on one of life's greatest experiences. But they simply don't see it like that, and we must accept their choice.

If you've already talked to them ...

... and it went well, then congratulations. You have negotiated a very tricky experience with grace and tact. Hopefully, your bond with your children is stronger than ever.

Bear in mind that they now know how you feel, and you don't need to remind them. It can be tempting to refer back to your big discussion. Avoid the temptation.

And you might want to reinforce the bond with your children, by reassuring them that you love them as much as ever and letting them know how proud you are of them. However well you think the discussion went, they may still be feeling a bit unsettled by it.

You have taken a big step on your journey towards peace and acceptance of your grandchildless state, though you may still have times of sadness and regret. Keep moving forward.

... and it did not go well. Firstly, I'm sorry. I am sure you meant well, and did the best you could.

You may be in any one of a wide range of situations now, from mild awkwardness between you and them to total estrangement.

Whichever it is, it can't hurt to apologise. Tell them how sorry you are it turned out this way, that you didn't mean to upset them and that you want to make amends.

It hardly needs saying that you won't raise the thorny issue of no grandchildren with them again. They'll have heard you, loud and clear. To go back over it is likely to fan the flames of discord, just as they are dying down.

Hopefully any coolness or rift will mend over time. Be patient.

And as always, if the situation seems bleak then counselling may be helpful, at least while you work to get your relationship back on track. Good luck.

Talking to acquaintances and strangers

Finally, let's consider that thorny and recurrent issue of what to say to people you hardly know, or have just met, when they ask if you have grandchildren.

This can be a real problem. For a long time, I tried to avoid social situations where I thought I'd be asked this. In fact I became quite reclusive, and I don't think I'm alone in this.

Eventually I came to realise that most people are only asking because it seems like a polite and safe topic. The reality is that other people are much less interested in us than we might think.

I was probably experiencing something called the "spotlight effect". This is a psychological term for the belief that people are much more interested in us, and notice what we do much more, than is actually the case. We all go through life as if there's a spotlight trained on us, which makes us the centre of attention. However, everyone else has a spotlight on them too!

Even some horrible experience that involved us and that has seared itself into our memory is likely to have been completely forgotten by everyone else who witnessed it. They are all much too absorbed in their own lives to care.

So if someone asks if we have grandchildren they are probably only making polite conversation, and whatever we reply they won't particularly mind or even remember.

Much of the discomfort in this scenario comes from the recurring sense that we've been caught on the hop and just don't have anything appropriate to say. So the first thing is to work out ahead of time what our answer is going to be.

We can of course just say "No". But if a bald negative response is too uncomfortable for us (and it's true that it might raise an eyebrow or cause an awkward silence), then we can try other responses, like -

"Not yet"

"No. I love my dog/cat/travel plans/houseplants though. Do you have those?"

"I'm too busy/young for grandchildren"

Or smile, ignore the question and change the subject!

You can of course think up something else that works for you. Experiment till you find an answer that you can trot out without much thought or discomfort, then practise using it. It'll get easier, I promise.

Talking to people about our lack of grandchildren can seem like an insurmountable problem at times. The more pain we are experiencing ourselves because of the issue, the harder it can be to cope with discussing it.

But it can be done. We need to keep reminding ourselves that it matters much more to us than anyone else; that practice makes progress, when it comes to navigating social situations; and that we can have a close and loving relationship with our children, whether or not we choose to tell them about our grandchildless journey.

CHAPTER NINE

WHAT TO DO WITH ALL THE STUFF

Our motto – *"The memories are in me, not in things."*

The shawl you were wrapped in at your christening. The hand-carved crib that's been in your family for generations. The quilt your mother made. The boxes and boxes of your children's baby clothes, toys, books and puzzles that you've "saved" for the grandkids.

Do you have any stuff like this? So many of us do. We've kept sentimental items from the past, and then collected more things in the expectation of passing them on at the right moment.

And now, we are facing the facts. That moment is never going to arrive.

It's surprising how much distress we can experience as a result. Items from the past are portals to another life. We pick up a babygro, perhaps the one our child wore on the way home from the hospital, and we're transformed for a moment into new mothers. Anxious or tired perhaps but full of happiness and hope for the future.

We leaf through a much-loved book and remember so vividly the feel of a little child sitting in our lap as we read to them. Or we put our hand on the crib and relive the times spent rocking a fretful baby.

We've also kept the expensive items, hoping to make life easier for our cash-strapped child as they became a parent. Maybe the Lego, the train set or the rocking horse. It cost a lot of money, we reason. Can't let go of that.

Some things involve other people, too. Heirlooms that have been passed from one generation to the next or an item given by a beloved grandparent. Baby clothes knitted by an aunt. You know the kind of thing.

(By the way, I am not referring here to items from your children that you are saving *for yourself*. That's fine – most of us have photos and boxes of memorabilia. I'm talking about stuff you've been saving or acquiring *for your grandchildren*.)

Trixie says -

"I have a child's rocking chair in my bedroom. It was mine first, and then my children sat in it. The paintwork is worn but that kind of makes it even more special. I always intended to pass it on one day but right now it's just home to an old doll of mine. Looking at it makes me feel low – I should probably get rid of it, or at least put it in the attic, but somehow I can't."

And this is Vanessa's take -

"The books are so hard to part with. I guess it's the librarian in me. They're not even in good condition so I can't donate them. But I enjoyed reading to my kids so much, and I wanted to repeat that experience with their kids. Throwing books away feels like throwing away part of their childhood."

We can experience pain every time we look at the stuff. It's like a doom-laden reminder of our grandchildlessness. Even squirrelling it away in lofts, attics or basements doesn't help that much. It's still *there*, and we know it. Feng Shui experts tell us that hiding items in this way saps our life force, and they may have a point.

So. What do we do with it all?

First, we make absolutely sure that we have offered everything to our children. Make it very clear that this is their last chance to take any favourite items, and that you will be disposing of the rest quite soon. They may have assumed you'd be storing their old toys forever. If they are out of college and have their own place, even if that's still a room in your house – then they are old enough to take charge of their own stuff.

Then, we need to acknowledge what these things have meant to us and to our children.

They were important. Our children were genuinely attached to that stuffed elephant, to this chewed board book or to the puzzle they did over and over when they were four.

And so we developed attachment too. To the memories, to how our children once were, to the positive associations that still reside for us in that particular object.

However – it's an illusion. Our child no longer cares. (And I'm assuming now that they have already taken anything they really *do* care about. It's probably much less than you expected.)

In fact, our children no longer exist except in our memories. They're grown ups now. And we need to be grown up too.

***

Let's try to see the items objectively. Suppose you were to view similar things that another person had saved. Would they trigger the same deep emotions in you? Of course not, because they wouldn't have any emotional resonance for you. They'd just be old stuff.

And realistically, that's what many of your items are, too. Just old stuff.

For a start, clothes go out of fashion, and baby clothes in particular usually take quite a beating in the laundry process. If you did have a grandchild, would their parents *really* dress the child in those old clothes?

Books and toys that have been well-loved also take a beating. Paper get stained and germ-laden when sticky little fingers turn the pages of a book. Plush toys are a dusty haven for bacteria. Even items that look clean enough might not be safe. If you did have a grandchild, would you *really* expose them to such health risks?

Consider this, too. If a toy or book is in pristine condition, is that because your kid didn't actually enjoy it much? If a dress or a little suit looks unworn, maybe that's because your child found it stiff, uncomfortable or embarrassing to wear. In which case, is any other child going to like it any better.

And anything that's been in storage for 20+ years will have its own issues. However carefully you wrapped the items, did they give off a musty smell when you opened the box or picked them up? If so, they are no longer safe for babies and young children.

Maybe you have some wooden toys, or plastic ones. Plastic degrades over time. The chemicals that make plastic toys soft enough to play with can leak out over the decades. And standards for paint or varnish on wooden items can also change – yours might not be safe according to up-to-date legislation.

What about a treasured cot or crib? (I'm assuming you wouldn't dream of reusing an old mattress – we're talking about the wooden structure). Safety standards may have changed here, too. Spindles might be the wrong distance apart, or the mechanism for lowering the sides might not comply with current rules.

Above all, even if there *was* a grandchild - parents want to create their own memories for their own children. They may appreciate the offer of a (new!) pram or stroller, or (new!) baby clothes. They may love gifts of (you guessed it – new) toys and books.

But there's every chance that they just wouldn't want your treasures. Trying to force your taste or your memories onto someone else is a losing proposition and can often lead to bad feeling and distance between people, however kindly meant.

So look at everything you've kept with a critical eye. Try, really try, to make decisions based on the above criteria.

If you do, you'll likely now have two categories of stuff to deal with -

Things that are safe and still usable, and

Things that no child should be exposed to.

Let's consider them in turn.

ACTION POINT – The rest of this chapter is one big action point. Take it gently, but do go ahead with it if you possibly can. It's a big step forward on the journey to peace and acceptance.

Category 1 – Things that are usable

This is usually the easier group of objects to cope with. The stuff may have resale value, which means you can donate, sell online and so forth if you want to.

First though I want to address one particular category of stuff, and that is items you've bought specifically for a future grandchild. Perhaps you are in the habit of strolling down the baby aisles in shops, or visiting specialist children's stores, and picking up bits and pieces that take your fancy? Maybe you even have a special storage space for these kinds of things?

If so, you need to stop doing that. Do not walk down those aisles or visit those shops any more. Instead, treat yourself to new clothes or makeup; buy some plants for the garden; go our for a special meal once a month, or set up a direct debit to a beloved charity. But *stop buying new stuff for a baby or small child.*

The good news is that these items make perfect donations to charity shops/ thrift stores. They are easy to sell and command top prices, so the charity will really benefit from your generosity. And some impoverished young mother will be thrilled to have an item she couldn't otherwise have afforded.

Also, the stuff will be *used.* A baby will wear that adorable outfit or play with those toys. Isn't that better than them languishing in a box in your home?

Be brave here. If a miracle happens and you do get a grandchild after all, you can always go out and shop again. Meanwhile you'll be freeing yourself from things that can only weigh you down and cause you pain. It's win-win.

That's the deal with brand-new stuff. With everything else, you have various options. Sell or give away are the main two, but recycling or even throwing things out is also possible.

If it's a genuine antique, a local antique dealer might be interested. Remember that current legal safety standards apply to anything that may be used by babies or children, though.

Otherwise online selling is always a possibility, via eBay for example. Prepare yourself to be surprised at how little your stuff is worth!

Giving saleable items in good condition to a charity to sell is always a great thing to do. Someone else who actually wants it, and maybe couldn't afford one new, gets to own and use it. A very worthwhile cause gets some money to further its good work. And you get a lovely glow from doing something wholly admirable. It's win-win all round.

You could also list on freecycle or Craigslist or a similar website. Be prepared for time-wasters.

Someone in the wider family might want an item, though do try to avoid guilt-tripping them into taking anything. But if there's somebody who you know has an interest in family history, or antiques or vintage items, it's worth a try.

Next, you could consider upcycling, the trendy term for transforming old stuff into newer-looking stuff. In particular, you might think about a change of use.

For instance, a cot or child's bed could become a small garden bench. A crib might turn into a planter. You could make patchwork from children's clothing, or a quilt.

BEWARE. It's all too easy to persuade yourself that you will get round to these projects one day – and then the items continue to sit in your house, sabotaging your progress. Also, however much you transform something, part of you still knows what it used to be. Can you truly escape from the memories this way? I doubt it.

Finally, two last options. You could recycle. Nothing wrong with that.

Or, you could just throw the item away. In these eco-conscious times some people will doubtless consider that sacrilege. But in the circumstances, if it's just too hard for you to deal with the stuff in any other way – I say go for it. Find some other route to reducing your carbon footprint, and put that thing in the bin.

***

Category 2 – Things that no child should be exposed to

Now, it's time to deal with everything else.

Be realistic and honest. If you're not 100% sure that something is safe, it has to go.

Take a deep breath.

You are going to dispose of these items, and this is hard. No giving them away to someone who "might need them", or dumping them on a charity shop or thrift store. They'll just be thrown out by someone else anyway and disposing of useless donations is a burden charities can do without.

It's our stuff, so it's our responsibility.

Do the following on the day your rubbish collection is due. That way you can't change your mind.

And if you really have kept *everything*, then you may need to break this project down into smaller tasks. So, tackle baby clothes this week, toddler clothes next week, soft toys the week after and so on.

Right, here we go.

Choose a quiet time when you won't be disturbed. Get a camera or your phone, a bin bag, and a box of tissues. Bring the items you're going to discard to a neutral venue – for example, the living room or the garden, rather than your child's old bedroom.

Take photos of everything. Hold the clothes one last time, and remember when your child wore them. Look through the books and recall how this story made your toddler laugh, or that one provoked an interesting conversation with your six-year-old. Stack the bricks together and knock them down, just as your baby once did.

You can thank each thing for its importance in your child's life, and in yours. Either say your thanks out loud, or consciously think it. For instance, "Thank you for being my son's beloved bedtime storybook when he was three. You helped him go to sleep night after night, and that was a big help to me too."

It might seem a bit silly, but expressing our gratitude in this way can aid us in letting go. Give it a try.

And then, say goodbye to each one. Fold the clothes, close the book, and lay them gently in the rubbish sack.

Of course, going through this process is very likely to result in you crying. That's OK. It's normal! Let the emotions out! Use the tissues. (But if you are really becoming very distressed, it's also OK to stop for now and try again later. Perhaps you are just not ready yet – there will be other opportunities.)

Remember our motto. **The memories are in you, not in the objects**. You have the photos to remind you. It's time to let the things go.

When you've finished, tie the top of the bag and go straight out to put it in the dustbin or garbage can. Come straight back into the house.

Now, make yourself a comforting beverage. Whatever works for you – lemonade, tea, coffee, or even a glass of wine.

If you need to upload your photos to your computer, do that now. Otherwise put them in a folder on your phone labelled "baby memories" or something similar. If you're as paranoid about losing files as me, back them up! They will always be there, and you can revisit them from time to time if you really need to.

Breathe deeply, and congratulate yourself on completing a very difficult job.

In the next few days, be gentle and kind to yourself if you find you are feeling low. You've accomplished an important step on your journey to peace and acceptance of your life without grandchildren. Well done.

On the other hand, you may find this was a cathartic experience, and you feel lighter and less burdened straight away. If so, that's fantastic.

If there's still stuff left over, repeat this process as many times as it takes. Good for you!

This process can be tough, and this chapter of the book will be a challenge for some. But it is an important step in becoming your new self. You'll no longer be shackled to the past and distressed by endless reminders of what might have been. Now you are freer to move on and explore exciting new options.

Let's look forward with hope, not backward with regret.

CHAPTER TEN

MEANING

Our motto – "We create our own meaning in life."

As we come to terms with what's happening to us, we may find ourselves wondering about the meaning of our lives. This might be a new experience. In the past, our children, jobs, family and friends probably gave us the sense of connection and purpose that all humans crave. But now, our kids are grown, perhaps retirement looms or has arrived and our social circle may have shrunk.

Let's be honest here. Grandchildren provide their grandparents with instant meaning. The family is continuing, we've passed on our genes in the most direct way possible and we can look forward to providing the younger generations with support for as long as we're able.

And we can enjoy all the pleasures of having young children around us once more, this time without the burden of too much responsibility. The natural cycle of life goes on and we're a significant and useful part of it.

We the grandchildless, on the other hand, need to create our own meaning. That can be challenging, but the good news is – it *can* be done.

GUIDE TO NO GRANDCHILDREN

We've already considered the genetic link we have with other members of the family. Our siblings' grandchildren seem a particularly likely source of satisfaction here. Why shouldn't they have doting great-aunts and great-uncles? Then there are cousins, friends and godchildren – any of them might also have small children in their families.

If you really do want to be around children and none present themselves, then the local maternity unit, playgroup, nursery school, forest school, primary school, Guides and Scouts etc. etc. are often crying out for volunteers.

So if it's substitute grandkids we want, there is likely to be a way to access them.

But let's move on from quasi-grandchildren. Many of us will find it too difficult to be constantly reminded of what we don't have. We want something else. And there are plenty more sources of meaning to be found.

What most people need are activities that give us purpose and structure in our daily lives. There are exceptions to this – if you have a very philosophical or spiritual approach to life, for example, you may find it's more than enough for you to appreciate the world around you, meditate, or spend time in prayer.

But many of us do well with some structure and a sense of having an aim or goal. If we feel these things are currently lacking, now is the time to take stock and consider what will work for us going forward.

Here are some ideas. Of course, these lists are in no ways exhaustive. There are dozens, no, hundreds of other possibilities!

Helping others

We've already touched on doing something for charity. This can be a fantastically meaningful thing to occupy you. But you can help others without it being within the formal structure of a charitable organisation.

Maybe you have a neighbour who'd appreciate a little help. Someone elderly or disabled, or a single mother struggling to cope. Perhaps you could get some shopping for them sometimes when you go to the supermarket. When you're pruning your roses, maybe you could offer to do theirs, too. Could it be that the seven year old who makes all that noise is behind with his reading and could do with a patient adult to help him along with his studies?

Maybe pets are your thing. Dog walkers are extremely sought after. You could do it for free or earn a little cash – your choice. You could offer a pet-sitting service for people going on holiday (they often want their plants watering, too.) You could take up breeding animals – anything from poodles to koi carp.

Teaching is also an invaluable skill and if you have something to share with local groups it should be easy to find a role. Here in the UK, U3A (University of the Third Age) is always looking for people to take classes, and the Women's Institute loves to have guest speakers.

You do not have to have any formal teaching qualifications for this kind of position, just experience and enthusiasm for your subject. I'm sure similar organisations exist in most other countries, too.

Passing on our life skills and wisdom; making life a little easier for someone who is in difficulties; knowing that you are making a difference to your fellow humans. Very little is more meaningful than that.

ACTION POINT – Think about whether it would add meaning to your life to help someone else. If so, start being open to possibilities.

Creativity

You could write (that's what I'm doing, after all!). Poetry, journaling, short stories, non-fiction, the novel you've always meant to get around to, or your life story.

You could paint, draw, sketch, do sculpture or pottery or photography. You could knit, crochet or stitch. There's upholstery, woodwork, jewellery-making and calligraphy.

You could make music or write music, join an amateur theatricals group or a choir, learn a new musical instrument, dance, become a DJ (no, it's not too late!)

Gardening can be wonderfully creative, and so can redecorating your home.

This is only scratching the surface of what's possible. All of these activities and hundreds more allow us to express ourselves. And isn't this part of the essence of being human? What can be more meaningful than that?

ACTION POINT – you could choose to reactivate an old hobby or start something fresh. Experiment till you find the one that scratches your creative itch!

But maybe creativity isn't your thing, so how about ...

Travel

Travel is a predictable thing to do once the children have left home, especially if you're recently retired. Always assuming your health is up to it and there isn't, you know, a global pandemic going on.

But predictable doesn't mean bad. The opportunity to travel, whether abroad or in our home country, is a wonderful privilege of modern life.

Just think of all those people in centuries gone by who never strayed from their villages. Consider how narrow their world view must have been compared with ours.

If you have the travel bug and you can afford to go, then good for you! Travel can provide structure, excitement and adventure, as well as something to look forward to. Those certainly add meaning to existence. As does the chance to see how people in other places live their lives (assuming we don't spend our whole vacation time in tourist enclaves.)

There are ways to "get away" even if the purse strings are tight. Could you stay with family or friends, or maybe swap accommodation with someone? Even day trips can be a treat, especially if they coincide with another purpose – visiting a museum for example, enjoying beautiful scenery or paddling in the sea.

And if you do manage to get abroad, then learning a new language can be a wonderful focus. It's also extremely good for our brains. Don't believe those old stories about there being a "critical time" to learn a language, after which it's too late. That just isn't true – you might never sound like a completely native speaker but you can still make excellent progress and become fluent if you want to put the time in.

ACTION POINT – think about how you could fit some travel into your life, even if your plans are modest.

Money making

For many of us, thinking about money is fundamentally stressful. There never seems to be enough – "Too much month at the end of the money" as the saying has it. Or, paying the bills and balancing the cheque book (or its modern equivalent) are chores we'd rather avoid. Even people who are comfortably off suffer money concerns.

So making money at this stage of our lives might not seem much fun. We may still be working, though we are probably past the point in our careers where we can expect much in the way of promotion and salary increases. Or we might already be retired, and concerned about the purchasing power of our pensions.

However, for some people making money can be a fun and enjoyable challenge. People who have been the primary homemaker in a family can relish the chance to get out into the world and start earning again. Or, people who have retired from a profession can find they miss the structure of work and set up as freelances or consultants.

It may not be too late to retrain for an entirely new career. For example, in my own field of counselling and psychotherapy, maturity is a great asset. It's normal to start the training in your forties or fifties, and even later in some cases.

A hobby could turn into a small business, maybe by chance – people love your sponge cakes or handmade earrings so much, you find you can start charging for them.

You might take up a new occupation that attracts payment. For example, writing reviews online, selling articles or short stories to magazines, dog walking, reselling on big online platforms. The internet has opened up a world of possibilities but traditional routes to extra money are still out there too.

Making our lives easier or more enjoyable by getting control of our finances and then boosting them can result in less stress and more spending power. Definitely meaningful!

ACTION POINT – make sure you are in control of your finances, then consider if you would enjoy trying to boost your income; or even if you'd enjoy a change of career.

Games and Sports

One of the best things we can do for ourselves is keep physically and mentally sharp. We'll touch on this again in the section on self care.

If you have a sport you used to love, and it's not too strenuous for you now, then why not go back to it? Nothing is off limits if you're in good shape physically, though you might like to run it past your doctor if you have concerns about any aspects of your health.

Here are some ideas for those of us in middle age and older.

All forms of walking are excellent. Swimming, tennis and golf are classics of course, but how about table tennis, badminton, yoga, dancing, Tai Chi, cycling, bowls, boules, walking football, croquet, archery, water aerobics or orienteering? That list might be exhausting to read but it isn't exhaustive – I'm sure there are plenty more I haven't mentioned.

If physical activity isn't for you, then how about the more intellectual side? Sitting-down games can be very beneficial for our mental fitness.

Crosswords and sudoku are available in almost every newspaper and can provide a stimulating activity over your breakfast, or a challenge that you can dip into on and off throughout the day.

Card games are wonderful. How about bridge, whist, or poker? You may have some favourites you remember from childhood – I used to play Gin Rummy with an old aunt, for example.

Then there are countless board games. There's the king of them all, chess. Old classics like Scrabble, Monopoly, Pictionary and Risk, and some of the new generation too, like Wingspan, Azul and 7Wonders – did you know there's been a revival in playing board games, and they are currently hip? There are even cafes where you can play them while you sip your latte.

There is also an amazing world of computer games to explore. The number of silver surfers who are also online gamers is increasing rapidly every year. Why not have a go at Candy Crush or Animal Crossing, create civilisations in Forge of Empires or adopt a new identity as an elf and play World of Warcraft?

ACTION POINT – Don't forget the fun to be had from sports and games at any age.

Education

The concept of education as a lifelong pursuit is a noble one. There is absolutely no reason why we should stop learning at 16, 18, 21 or any other arbitrary age. Learning something new, or deepening our existing knowledge, is fun, life-enhancing and very good for us.

If you didn't complete you schooling or never had the chance to go to college or university, consider whether you could do it now. Mature students of any age are generally welcome in further and higher education. Part-time study is usually possible. You can often gain your school-leaving qualification, a diploma or a degree via a distance learning organisation if you can't get to a campus.

Your local area might provide Adult Education classes in all kinds of areas – from maths and English, via foreign languages, art appreciation and local history, to woodwork, cake decorating and painting. And much more.

Here in the UK, the University of the Third Age (U3A) is set up for retired people and offers a wide range of classes and events all over the country. I took beginner's Spanish with them and it was a hoot! They are always looking for tutors so if you have a skill to offer, you could set up your own class through them.

If you're self-motivated you could also create your own study programme. Perhaps you've always wanted to read classic literature but never got further than Pride and Prejudice, for example? Why not aim to read all six of Jane Austen's novels, and supplement that by going online to join GoodReads, where you'll find read-a-longs, reviews, suggestions for further reading and all kinds of support.

YouTube is another great educational resource. You can watch specialists in any field giving lectures and being interviewed. YouTube is also particularly good for language learning, as you can easily find native speakers and improve your accent.

ACTION POINT – It's never to late to learn. See if there's a topic that interests you and if so, go for it!

FINAL ACTION POINT – look for all kinds of ways to add meaning and joy to your life. Not having grandchildren does NOT have to be the end of everything for us.

This Final Action Point is the most significant of all. Move forward into a new phase of happiness and fulfilment. You deserve it.

CHAPTER ELEVEN

SELF CARE

Our motto – *"Love yourself; there's only one you."*

When we were little, someone else looked after us. Part of the task of growing up is to take on this responsibility for ourselves. And in many practical ways, that's obvious and straightforward – as a rule, when we are adults we no longer expect another person to bathe us or cook all our food, for example.

But when it comes to looking after our health, mental and physical, we might not be quite as self-sufficient as we think.

There are good reasons for some of this. A health problem may require professional expertise to treat effectively. Modern jobs often put physical strains on us that we are not designed to withstand long-term (for example, sitting at a computer for hours at a time, like I'm doing now!). The stresses of our lives make it all too easy to reach for unhealthy ready meals, alcohol and the TV remote control.

Also, society exists to support us when we're struggling. And so relying on others for support and comfort in times of emergency is automatic, and often effective.

But all of this leaves a blurred area where we *could* do more to look after ourselves, but may not know how. Or, we do know how, but we just don't want to do the work. It's very understandable, though we all know it may not be in our best interests.

We've already explored a lot of the emotional aspects of self care in the previous chapter.

So the aim of this chapter is to suggest some ways in which we can look after ourselves better physically and spiritually. Please remember that these are only ideas; I'm not telling you what to do.

And if you're wondering what all this is doing in a book about not having grandchildren, it's a fair question. Feel free to move on to the next chapter if it's not for you.

However, I would say that the stronger and more robust we are, mentally, physically, and spiritually, the better we can cope with whatever problems life throws in our path. And so I do think this could be useful information, even if it's just an opportunity to reflect a little on your current lifestyle.

Of course, entire books have been written about these topics. You may already be familiar with some of them. This book is primarily about our experience of not having grandchildren, so there is only room to scratch the surface here.

It's your body, your mind and your health. I truly believe that, deep down, we each know what we need. Sometimes it takes a little digging to work it out, that's all.

Let's start with our physical health.

What we eat and drink

You've heard it all before, I'm sure. Maybe you're a serial dieter, or you know you're consuming too much alcohol, or you've been told to cut down on fatty food but you can't resist it.

"Give up sugar, eat more fibre, drink no more than three units of alcohol per day (or is it two?)". And so on.

I don't believe there's anything intrinsically wrong with eating and drinking however we like. This is not a moral issue – we're not weaklings if we overindulge. In fact, we humans are hardwired to eat as much fatty and sugary food as we can get our hands on, because those are full of calories and for most of human history, calories were in short supply.

But equally, it's clear that some foods are better for our health than others. I'm sure I hardly need to say that being overweight or drinking too much alcohol is not good for our bodies.

So what we can do, is make intelligent choices.

Here's a good tip – *don't give things up, switch them out*. This works in all kinds of contexts, and it's an excellent psychological strategy here.

Nobody likes to give anything up. It triggers feelings of loss, poverty, lack of status and all kinds of other unpleasant things. But we are usually fine with swapping out an old thing for a new thing. "Fair exchange is no robbery," as the old saying goes.

For instance, don't give up your mid-afternoon slice of cake and then sit dreaming of cream and sponge while your tummy rumbles. Instead, exchange it for some fresh fruit. And if that sounds dull, think about eating a lovely, juicy mango, with its mouthwatering orange flesh – or a sweet medjool date or some thin-skinned, sun-kissed grapes. Something like that will satisfy your sugar craving for sure, and be far healthier and lower-calorie too.

It is also completely legitimate to swap the less healthy version for a more healthy version. For example, given that refined sugar and salt are both very bad for us, it follows that low-sugar biscuits/cookies are likely to be better for you than high-sugar ones, and low-salt crisps/chips are better than salty ones. And if you haven't tried unsalted nuts, give them a go. They're yummy!

When it comes to drinks of all kinds, the same principle applies.

For example, while two or three cups of tea or coffee per day are probably fine, if you find yourself drinking ten a day it's time to act. Swap some of those caffeinated cups for decaf, or herbal tea. Also, be aware that our ability to metabolise caffeine diminishes as we age. So if you're often anxious or jittery it might be worth examining your caffeine consumption to see if that might be the culprit.

Here's a confession. I just drink hot water some of the time. It might sound bizarre, but it gives me most of what I want – a break from my current occupation while I get up and go into the kitchen, then the ritual of boiling the kettle and making the drink, plus the comfort of holding a mug full of hot liquid, and sipping from it. Psychological tricks like this can be so useful!

With alcohol, it often helps to make sure you're drinking as much water as booze. Start your evening with a glass of water (bear in mind that you might actually be thirsty, so the water may be just what your body needs). Then have another glass of H2O after every one of wine, beer or whatever. You're not restricting the amount you drink in any way – and yet, since your body is well-hydrated, the effect of the booze will be less damaging. And you might find you *are* drinking less alcohol without really meaning too. Clever, isn't it?

As for carbonated beverages - fizzy drinks, soda, cola, pop, seltzer, or whatever, they're known as in your local area – there are two main problems with those. The first is that they may contain caffeine, in some cases large amounts of it. The obvious answer here is to switch to the caffeine-free version, though if you are used to drinking several cans or bottles per day, go slowly with this to avoid problematic caffeine withdrawal. Maybe start with substituting just one or two cans a day.

The other issue is the large amounts of sugar involved. A well-known brand of cola contains 35 grams of sugar per can. That is NINE teaspoons of sugar. This level of sugar intake will play havoc with anyone's insulin levels, so switching to the low cal version will be a massive benefit. But again, doing this gradually will be less of a shock to your system and easier to stick with, as long as you keep going.

So there's my take on food and drink. You get the idea. For any foodstuff or beverage that you know is unhealthy, switch to a healthier version. You don't need to do this all at once, either. Maybe just change one thing a week; but if you stick with it, in a couple of months you'll be making a significant, positive difference to what you're consuming.

Psychologically, you'll be much more content with exchanging one thing for another than with denying yourself. Try it and see for yourself.

ACTION POINT – Don't give it up; exchange it for something better.

Why we overeat and drink too much

Clearly, it's not just hunger and thirst at play here. So the next step is to see if you can work out what triggers your desire for a particular food or drink. If it is genuine hunger or thirst, then of course that's legitimate.

But very often it's something else. What might it be? Sadness or anger? Boredom? Loneliness?

If you can't tell, you could try keeping a diary for a week or so of everything you eat and drink. Record your emotional state next to the items you're consuming. Then see if a pattern emerges – for example, you eat healthily most of the time but then you graze mindlessly while watching TV.

At those times, try substituting an activity for eating. You'll be swapping again, you see, not giving anything up. "The devil makes work for idle hands", as we've been told. And we don't want that work to be opening a box of chocolates.

So if you're bored or sad, and find yourself reaching for a bag of chips or a doughnut, think about what else you could be doing.

One idea that has a lot of potential is a craft of some kind. If your hands are occupied with crochet, knitting, card-making or something similar, they aren't delving into the cookie jar or biscuit barrel. Those sorts of activities are very compatible with watching TV or listening to music, too, so there's no need to give up your entertainment of choice.

Or you could take pride in your hands and manicure your nails. Or try armchair exercising – it can be surprisingly effective for your body's muscle tone, and it's something even people with reduced mobility can do successfully.

Yet another idea is a revamp of your living space. Make a list of little jobs that need attending to, or plan a redecoration. Break the jobs into very small bits so it's easy to see yourself making progress and write it all down. When loneliness or boredom strikes, look at your list and see if you can't tick off one or two activities in the next hour or so.

A laptop computer or mobile phone can keep your hands occupied too. You could reply to your emails or pay your bills. Not fun but useful and constructive. Or for fun, you can engage with social media (in a constructive way) or play online games. Much more healthy to move bits of candy round a screen, rather than putting them in your mouth!

ACTION POINT – See if you can work out the emotion behind overindulging, then find a better thing to do.

Physical Fitness

Yes, I know – yawn. So many messages bombard us. Take ten thousand steps a day, go to the gym, use the stairs and walk whenever we can. But suppose we have busy lives, depression or an arthritic knee?

We are grown-ups, and I repeat - what we do to our bodies is our own business. I'm not here to give you any specific advice on this, other than if you're over 50 and/or have an underlying health issue, please always check with your doctor if you plan on taking up a new exercise or diet regime.

What I will say, though, is that becoming physically fitter is likely to make you happier overall. And that taking baby steps is vastly better than taking no steps at all.

The greatest benefit to increasing your level of activity comes right at the beginning. So for example, if you've been largely inactive and currently take fewer than 1000 steps a day, switching that up to 2000 steps will likely have a noticeable impact on your overall health.

Get a step counter, if possible. You don't need to spend a lot of money. In fact you may have a perfectly usable one on your mobile phone already.

You do NOT need to go full out for the 10,000 right away, and doing so is likely to result in soreness, discouragement and giving up. Same thing with suddenly digging the garden for hours, or dusting off that old squash racquet for a vigorous (and potentially dangerous) game. Baby steps!

There are more ideas for physical activities in the section on Games and Sports in Chapter 9.

That's it for this topic, as there isn't the space here to go into more detail. Plenty of info is available in numerous other books, articles, and online.

ACTION POINT – Take baby steps on your road to improved health. Small amounts of improvement, repeated over time, add up to big progress.

Spirituality

Some of you will have a religious belief, and may belong to a church, or other faith organisation. Throughout history people have turned to a higher power when they are struggling in life. If this describes you, I only want to say - may you find the comfort and encouragement you are seeking.

Others may not have that bedrock of faith and might wonder what this vague term "spirituality" has to do with them.

The word used to be used only in a specific religious sense, but these days it tends to refer to any search for deep meaning and values in our lives.

Yes, it *is* quite vague! I'm using it here in relation to our quest for meaning and purpose in our lives. That can be important if it isn't going to be through the continuation of our direct family line via grandchildren, and all that they would have brought us.

For me, two aspects of spirituality seem particularly relevant to our situation.

The first is our personal experience of being here in the world right now – how we can enrich that experience and gain satisfaction and meaning from it. I'll call this *Being Present*.

And the second is about how we can relate to other people in a way that deepens our appreciation of them, and enriches our lives as a result. I'm calling this *Connection*.

Once again, if this is all too New Age for you, please feel free to move on to the next chapter. I won't be offended!

Being Present

I have great admiration for those who can be still and simply enjoy whatever comes along. Perhaps they are using a Buddhist approach, for example, which includes a desire to open ourselves to life as it is and accept it wholeheartedly.

In particular, we can concentrate fully on whatever we are doing at a particular time. If we're eating, we can focus on the textures and tastes of the food in our mouths. If we are gardening, we can take time to notice the feel of the earth beneath our fingers and the sun on our back.

The weather is something we often largely ignore, unless it's causing us inconvenience in some way. But it can be a source of fascination. As we feel the wind blowing our hair or watch rain lashing against a window, it's a great way to notice life as it is, right now.

The exhortation to "smell the roses" is used so often that it may have come to seem trivial, but there is great wisdom in allowing ourselves to slow down and take in a beautiful sunset, the taste of a piece of ripe fruit, or an inspiring piece of art.

Personally, I lived for some time in my twenties without any means of heating the water in my home. So today the simple act of turning on a tap and having hot water gush out never ceases to give me a sense of pleasure and luxury!

We can all aim to include this kind of enjoyment of the everyday in our lives. Much of daily life *is* fairly mundane, after all. The more fun and satisfaction we can derive from simple things, the better.

You might like to explore the practice of meditation. This is not anything difficult or special. We can start simply by being aware our breathing, without trying to control it. As we do so, we can notice the thoughts that arise in our minds (there will almost certainly be plenty of them). We let them pass through us without judgement.

That's basic meditation in a nutshell, and when practised regularly it's been shown to have remarkable beneficial effects on the body. If you are interested in taking it further, you'll find plenty of resources, either through books, online or maybe in your local community.

ACTION POINT – Notice what's happening right at this moment, and take time to smell the roses.

Connection

Are you a good listener? Do people tell you important things about their lives, knowing they'll get a sympathetic hearing?

Or perhaps you're good at doing what needs to be done for others. You can tell when someone's struggling and you're willing to step in and help.

Or maybe you're a great communicator or teacher. You can express ideas and concepts in a way that others can hear.

Alternatively, you are not afraid to admit when you don't understand something and you can learn from others.

All of these are ways of connecting. "Only connect!", as E.M. Forster famously told us.

We need relationships (mostly human ones, but pets can provide the right sort of connection too) in order to be happy and fulfilled, and those relationships stand or fall on the degree of connectedness we can achieve.

There is a lot about effective communication in Chapter 8, How to Talk to People. That focuses mainly on talking, and how we can both get our ideas across and also understand where other people are coming from. But here I'm casting the net wider and including all kinds of ways we can create and deepen relationships.

So my suggestion is to consider the quality of the connections you have, and ways in which you can harness your strengths to improve them. Also, you could look for new ways to connect with people. The Internet provides a wealth of opportunities, for a start.

ACTION POINT – Only connect. Look for ways to create new connections, and deepen the ones you already have.

CHAPTER TWELVE

MONEY AND LEGACY

Our motto – *"You can't take it with you, but you can send it on ahead."*

This chapter will cover several topics -

- What we do with our money and property while we are still here
- The same question, but after we're gone
- What else do we leave behind us?

Some of us lead simple lives, earning a modest income and never accumulating much in the way of savings or possessions. Others are, in the eyes of the world, financially rich.

And most of us are somewhere in between. We don't have vast wealth to worry about but neither are the coffers bare. So, as the years pile up, our thoughts inevitably turn at some point to the age-old question – what will happen to all this when we're gone?

You might find the topic morbid or depressing and of course it's sad to contemplate the future in this way. But, if we don't think it through now we are liable to leave a mess for our children to clear up. That's not fair on them, especially at a time when they will be grieving.

Also, there is a lot of comfort and even happiness to be gained *right now* from working through these issues. You could benefit others, and yourself, while it's most useful to them and you're still able to enjoy the results. That can be a big plus in our later years.

So let's begin by considering what we might be doing with our money and other property today.

Paying off all our debts

It goes without saying that we should be aiming to be debt-free at this time in our lives, if at all possible. If we have debts now they may outlive us, and that is one legacy we most certainly don't want to leave to our loved ones.

If we rent our home, we should be looking to ensure we can manage that rent on our pensions. If we're homeowners, the mortgage needs to be paid off. And now that our children have flown the nest, we hopefully no longer need loans for items such as cars or home improvements.

If you're in debt, please try to address this as a priority right now. It is beyond the scope of this book to address problems with debt, but there are free advice agencies that will help you if you're struggling.

ACTION POINT – Take a close look at your finances. If there are problems, especially debts, start taking action to fix it. Look for free debt advice services if necessary.

Now we can move on to ...

Downsizing, and gifting items

It's quite common these days for people to downsize their home at some point once the children have left. And for us as grandchildless people, there's an additional and very poignant reason to consider doing this. We now know our home is never going to be filled with grandchildren.

We're not going to be hosting huge holiday gatherings for our family, or sleepovers, or summer vacations with Grandma and Grandpa.

This can be a bitter pill to swallow as we gaze at our large dining table or wander round our spare bedrooms.

Moving to a smaller place removes a good deal of that pain. We don't have the sense of "if only" any more, at least not in relation to our home. We no longer have the space for lots of people and that's that.

Also, of course, it's much easier and cheaper to manage a smaller place. That's an important consideration later in life.

On the other hand, there is more to our family home than just space. There are happy memories here. We might feel we can cope with it, physically and financially, for many more years yet.

Maybe we've spent decades tending our garden and it's just reaching its mature beauty (like us?!). Our children might suddenly need to come home for a while. And property is an investment, so if we own it and are looking to sell, we need to consider what else we might do with the money we release (the extra funds could be a major plus, of course).

So this is a big decision that requires careful thought. No need to rush. I believe we usually know when the time is right, if we listen to our intuition.

ACTION POINT – sit down with a notebook and pen, and make a Pros v. Cons list regarding your current living situation. The results may surprise you!

If we do downsize, we will almost certainly need to find new homes for a lot of furniture and other household stuff. And as we found in the previous chapter, we might well discover that the next generation is not very interested in our treasures and heirlooms.

Fashions change, and never have they changed so radically as in the last few decades. Pick up an IKEA catalogue, or go online and have a look at contemporary furnishing styles.

Younger people mostly favour a streamlined look, with minimal clutter. It's highly probable that they do not share your taste. Also, they may be living in small homes or apartments themselves. They just don't have room for your cast-offs.

I know this can be a very painful realisation, but try not to take it personally. They are not rejecting *us* if they don't want our things!

Economic realities have changed. Furniture, crockery and so on used to be a big expense, but these days that kind of stuff is relatively cheap. We feel sentimentality for things that have been in our family for decades. But there was once a pressing economic need to pass items down the generations, and nowadays that need has largely gone.

So we can be empathic and cut our children some slack here. They don't want to be the only ones in their social circle whose homes are furnished with things that, to them, are dated and shabby. And as for real antiques, those are the preserve of rich old people. Probably not the vibe they're going for!

You may be able to sell some items. Charities will take anything in sound condition that meets current safety standards. Or someone else in the family might be interested. But you may have to face up to recycling or throwing away some things and that's a hard but necessary part of the journey.

The process we walked through in Chapter 9 is valid here, too. You are being brave when you rehome your stuff. It's emotionally tough, so treat yourself gently and congratulate yourself on a great job as you make progress. Good for you!

ACTION POINT – Start to evaluate the stuff in your home. Move your mindset towards being open to letting things go. Take opportunities as they arise to gift or rehome anything you don't need.

After we're gone

Your wishes, and the distribution of your estate, will be clear from the will you've had drawn up.

And if you're now thinking "Oh yes, must get round to doing that (or updating that) someday ..." then it needs to be top of your priority list. Seriously. Another thing our children don't need when they are grieving our passing, is to find out that we died intestate (didn't have a valid will) or hadn't updated it to reflect changed circumstances. It makes the whole process much, much slower, more expensive and generally more distressing for them.

There's no doubt that many of us would have done things differently if there had been grandchildren. Leaving money and/or property to our grown-up and very possibly middle-aged children can seem redundant. They are likely to be settled in careers and homes of their own and while it's no doubt nice for them to receive a windfall, it probably won't radically alter their lives.

For grandchildren it would have been different. They may have been at a stage of life where they could really use some cash. Student debt, buying a first car, climbing onto the housing ladder, getting married, setting up a business or even starting their own families – all of these are expensive activities.

So it's realistic to think carefully about how we want our estate to be distributed. Of course, I'm not for a moment suggesting we should disinherit our children – it may be illegal in your country to do that, for a start - and if it still seems right to leave everything to them, then of course that's the traditional solution and absolutely fine. It's also the simplest way to go.

But I believe it's also fine to at least consider leaving legacies for other family members, friends, and charities. And these might well constitute a larger slice of the pie than would have been the case if grandkids had been in the picture.

Think outside the box, and you could find a way to benefit others in a way you'd never considered. There can be satisfaction and joy in that.

ACTION POINT – MAKE A WILL. If you already have one, check that it still accurately reflects your wishes.

And so this leads us on to consider our ...

Legacy

There are two aspects to this. There's a family/genetic view of legacy and another that focuses more on who we have been and how we've left our mark on the world. Let's take these in turn.

Passing on our genes

This is one of the biggest deals associated with having no grandchildren, isn't it. The sense that after our children are gone, that's it for our family tree. Instead of a line of descendants stretching out into a misty future, there's a blank wall.

Jeff says -

> *"Yes, it has occurred to me that this will be the end of our family line, if Joel and Marissa remain childless. That saddens me sometimes. My mother traced the family back several centuries, and I have a framed print of the family tree. There's nobody very special in our*

family history, but still, it would have been good to think of the line continuing."

But is it really like this? Let's think this through logically.

Our child or children inherit half their genes from us, and half from their other parent. There are four grandparents. So a grandchild is only 25% "from us", genetically speaking.

We share half our genes with any full brother or sister. So their children (our nephews and nieces) are also 25% genetically linked to us. That's quite a lot, and certainly enough for us to feel that our genetic material is being carried into the future, surely?

Great nieces and nephews carry 12.5% shared genes, and so do first cousins. People you've never even met, perhaps!

OK, it's not as much or as direct as grandchildren. But think about anyone you know with grandchildren. Are those kids really that similar to their grandparents? Sometimes in my experience they're so different, you wonder if they are truly related at all!

So maybe the knowledge that other family members are also part of your family, and are carrying the legacy forward, can help.

It's only in recent times that "the family" has been such a small, nuclear group. In generations past it was a big ramshackle affair, encompassing all kinds of remote cousins and great aunts - a tribe, even. Think of it in this way, and you'll almost certainly see that you will live on in someone. It's not necessarily the end of "the family" after all.

Doing good and being remembered

Here is where we can have an impact, if we choose. Unlike the situation with grandchildren, this part of our legacy is under our control.

Many people remember a particular charity in their will. Often it relates to an illness someone in the family has been through. Or we

GUIDE TO NO GRANDCHILDREN

have a particular interest – we love animals, or we want to support the lifeboats because we live near the sea, for example.

If it isn't too painful, you might choose a charity that funds a child-related cause – an orphanage, a special care baby unit in your local hospital, or education in a developing country.

All this is great, of course, and it can be comforting to know that our legacy will help those organisations one day.

But even better - not only can we benefit a cause of our choice after we're gone, we can start *right now*.

Think of the money you might have spent on grandkids, if they'd existed. And then think how much good you could do with that money.

Maybe budget a proportion of your income for giving on a regular basis. Of course, it needs to be easily affordable for you. There is no need to scrimp in order to pay for this! But it doesn't matter how modest or large the sum is – it's the act of giving that rewards us.

Many charities interact with their sponsors in some way, especially if they are regular donors. You might get email updates on their work. Some have welcome packs. Or even a cuddly toy when you join!

Taking an interest in the progress of our chosen cause can be very good for our mental health. It takes us out of ourselves, and refocuses our attention on the wider world. It reminds us that others are suffering, too. And this kind of connection with society can be so useful as we get older.

Of course, it does not need to involve money. Many charities are crying out for volunteers to help them in all kinds of capacities. You might not need to leave home in order to do this – the internet provides all kinds of new roles.

You don't need to devote large amounts of time either. A few hours per week or even per month will be gratefully accepted by many organisations.

The variety of opportunities is huge. Do you have a specific skill, perhaps related to your current or former career, that you could share? Are you a good listener? Do you have a hobby that could benefit others? Excellent. Do a little research, pick your good cause and go for it!

***

Being remembered

And at the end of it all – will we be remembered? Few people achieve the kind of fame that echoes down the centuries. Then again, having grandchildren or not has very little to do with that.

Yes, we'll be remembered. By our children, and our wider family. By our friends. By anyone whose lives we've touched.

We have a great deal of control over *how* we are remembered. Will it be as a loving, generous friend and family member? As a good listener, or someone who was willing to pitch in and help out? Someone who willingly shared their wisdom when asked, but never dished out unwanted advice? Who accepted people as they were, but still always thought the best of them?

Or alternatively, will they recall us as bitter and unfulfilled, critical and unkind? Will they be glad to forget us, since we brought so little positivity into their lives?

It's up to us to make sure our later years are as fulfilling as possible, that we act with kindness, and that our general attitude is open, generous and loving. That's what others remember with affection and gratitude.

***

So, we've read the book and completed the exercises (well, most of them!). We've surveyed the scene, thought about our situation and drawn up our action plan. And we've made the decision. The years ahead will be meaningful, satisfying and fun.

Ready? Let's go!

RESOURCES

You won't be surprised to hear that there isn't much out there in the way of support for us.

However, there's one place that I can highly recommend. It's "A group for mothers who wish to be grandmothers but our grown children don't want, or can't have, children."

The group is called Grieving No Grandchildren, and it's on Facebook. You'll find it a safe, welcoming and caring place where women can express their feelings without fear of judgement or criticism. The group is private, so no risk of family members seeing what you post, and it is sensitively monitored by the woman who set it up.

Let's hope there is more of this kind of help in years to come.

Printed in Great Britain
by Amazon

27590478R10081